The Jacob Ladder

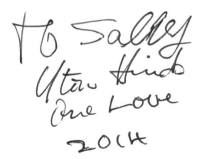

To Sally
Utan Hinds
One Love
2014

Irie Books
12699 Cristi Way
Bokeelia, Florida 33922

ISBN 10: 1-61720-197-9
ISBN 13: 978-1-61720-197-4
First Edition

10 9 8 7 6 5 4 3 2 1

This book was originally published in hardcover by Orchard
Books in 2001. A second edition was published by
Scholastic/Apple Paperbacks in 2003. Irie Books cover
design by NRK Designs, Bokeelia, Florida.

The Jacob Ladder

Gerald Hausman

with Uton Hinds

For Iya, who never lost faith in her children
and who always forgave Brother John

G. H. & U. H.

Chapter 1

They call me Tall T although my real name's Uton. I got the name Tall T because the letter T stands tall in the alphabet. Tall and slender and straight. Just like me, even though I'm only twelve years old.

There are four boys in my family, all tall. Tall and proud and a little shy, so they say. Then there are the girls, the twins, Merline and Maxine. Merline's tall and Maxine's short, but I'll have more to say about them later.

Johnny's the tallest and the eldest. Everyone in the neighborhood calls him Tall-y, except us. We call him Johnny.

Winston's my younger brother. His nickname's Bup, which he got by swimming like a worm (he's the worst swimmer in the family), so all of us kids started calling him Bup – you know, because he bupped around in the water. Bernel's the youngest brother. We call him Tonyskank, because he's always skanking, or joking around, with everybody.

The twins, Merline and Maxine, don't have any nicknames — that's a boy thing, I guess. But, anyway, Maxine's small and Merline's tall, and they're only seven years old, so it's hard to tell if they're going to be as tall as the rest of us.

Mama's a pretty tall lady too, but no one in our family calls her by any name except Iya. That's because whenever we used to cry out for her, she said we went, "Iya, Iya, Iya." So, the name stuck.

My father is the tallest person in Oracabessa, the town where we live in Jamaica. His nickname's Brother John, since he's sort of everybody's brother. But Brother John stands tall in other ways too. He's the town barber. The big lead rowboat man down at the docks when the banana boats come in. And he's also the head of the Jonkonnu band.

The only sorry thing about Brother John is that he's the unluckiest man at bone dice in the whole world. And, what's worse, he likes nothing better than to play them. Which makes him a little less tall, in my book. But that's neither here nor there.

When Brother John walks down the street, everybody looks up and waves, and nobody believes it when, after playing bones, Brother John changes around and starts acting like the devil. Some say it's really on account of his dressing up like the devil when he dances the Jonkonnu at Christmastime. They say he plays his part so well it makes him mad as a mongoose.

But I know the truth. It was a bowl of calaloo soup made Brother John into a madman. Yes, a bowl of calaloo soup turned our family upside down. One little bowl of calaloo soup, and, all of a sudden, I am the head of our house.

This is how it happened....

Chapter 2

Brother John comes home one afternoon from his rowing job down at the dock. Johnny and I are sitting on the porch enjoying the breeze.

"Tall T," Brother John says roughly, "carry come a bottle of white." He means 100-proof white rum. He hands me some money, and I run up the street to the little shop that sells rum. I buy him a bottle and I run back. He counts the change, careful as a clerk.

I say, "Brother John, me no thief you."

"No road so straight it not ziggy somewhere," he rumbles as he unscrews the top. What he means is, there's no road so straight it doesn't have a curve up ahead, and no son so straight he won't sneak a bit of change, now and then.

I am not like that, and he knows this. But he always counts out the change that I bring back.

Now he starts drinking rum, right out of the bottle. You wouldn't think anything that looks like water could mash up a man's mind – but white rum does just that. It's all right to use it as a medicine, I suppose. Iya puts it on my forehead when I'm running a fever. But that's not how Brother John uses it.

He tilts it up and drinks it down. Do you know how strong white rum is? You can light a fire with it, I'm telling you.

Then Brother John says, "Me go down to the dock and play some bone dice."

It's Friday, payday, and I know he's got a whole lot of money on him, and I also know that he's going to throw the bone dice – and lose all of it. Brother John's a man who's lucky in most things – except gambling.

We watch him—Johnny and I—as he walks down the road. At a distance we follow him to the Jacob Ladder. This is a cliff wall that goes down to the dockside. Long ago, before I was born, the banana men cut stairs in the cold clay. Coming up and going down, the Jacob Ladder is so steep, the men have to use the hanging fig vines to pull themselves up.

So, Brother John goes down the Ladder. We sit and wait for him in the shadow of the fig leaves. We listen to the bones rattle and to the dice man making his calls. We're wondering why can't Brother John win—just once? How come Iya lets him go do this? How come we can't stop him?

Well, nobody can stop a freight train or a hurricane or Brother John. He can lift a donkey off the ground and he can dance Jonkonnu all day long, and he can outtalk and outlaugh and outrage anybody who stands in his way.

After an hour or so, Brother John hauls himself back up the Ladder, his powerful arms winching him up. His feet, treading air like an angel, barely touch the stairs. We can see, though, it's no angel coming up the Ladder.

Then Johnny and I hide in the croton bushes of Mr. Hopson's Lunch Shop, which serves bun and cheese. We watch Brother John go up the road to Tank Lane where we live. The way he walks, with his long arms swinging and his hands balled up into fists, tells us he's heading for trouble.

"Remember the night," Johnny asks, "when he come home and throw money out of his pockets all over the table and the floor and everywhere?"

"I remember. It only happen once."

"Twice," Johnny reminds.

"He broke tonight," I add, watching Brother John stalk up the lamp-lit street.

Chapter 3

Tank Lane winds into the hills above the village, twists into the gloom of yards and fruit trees. It creeps up into the sweet, sweet hills of Oracabessa, which means golden head in Spanish. We follow Brother John as he goes up Tank Lane, his fists closed.

We figure he's got no more money, by the tight-fisted, hunch-shouldered way he's walking. We follow behind, quiet as mice.

I say to Johnny, "Oh-oh, he's heading into that obeah woman's house."

"The witch," Johnny whispers.

That's what she is: a witch. And I don't mean a mean person, I mean someone who casts spells for money. In Jamaica, we call it *obeah*. On other islands, it's voodoo.

Anyway, the obeah lady's name is Vera Watson, but everybody calls her Mama Poon. She's got a daughter named Lorita who's always feasting her eyes on Brother John. Looking at him, hungry. She's got a greedy green eye for any man, but mostly for Brother John.

Mama Poon's behind this, making Lorita flicker that hungry eye. And making Brother John look back at her with that wicked grin of his.

Johnny and I watch as Brother John stops in front of Mama Poon's house, which is right next door to ours.

We've lived next door to her all these years, and she's never cast a spell on us. Half of Oracabessa's been under her spell, one time or another. But, somehow, we've been spared.

Johnny says, "Look at that Mama Poon, just staring at Brother John."

She is sitting on her porch, smoking a cigarette. I can feel her eyes more than I can see them. They're smoldering like the ember at the end of her cigarette.

Then Brother John lurches around. He starts back down to our house.

"Him sleep it off," Johnny says.

But I don't think so. I see Lorita winking at him by the hedgerow that separates our yards. He stops again, scratching his head. Lorita smiles.

Brother John grunts, and starts toward our house. But he keeps looking back at Lorita. Then I hear Mama Poon laugh, just once.

Brother John staggers through our gate, leaving it wide open. He walks onto the verandah and opens the front door. For a moment his huge shadow darkens the doorway. Then he disappears inside.

Johnny and I squat down behind the croton bush.

With the front door open, we can see all the way to the back, where Iya is folding up the clothes that have dried on the line. The house is one big room with Iya and Brother John's bedroom separated from us kids by a partition wall. The rest of the house is open. Brother John, as we can see through the window, is grabbing at things like a giant crab. He's throwing clothes all around and rifling under the bed for his old cardboard suitcase.

"Him mad?" Johnny asks.

What now? I wonder.

Neither of us knows what's going on, or what's about to happen. "Him fixing to do something," Johnny says. From where we're hiding, I see Iya watching.

Watching and folding. She too can see into the house from back-a-yard.

Suddenly Brother John seems to fall out the front door. He drops something onto the porch with a loud thump – the busted old suitcase with the clothes sticking out at the edges.

We're scrunched down low, safe from Brother John's eyes. But he's looking all around just the same, as if he can feel us staring. Iya steps away from his view at the back door.

"Where him go with that suitcase?" Johnny whispers.

Brother John stares straight ahead like a zombie. He picks up his suitcase and walks off the porch. Same time, we squeeze into the crotons and disappear as he walks through the gate. He leaves it open, swinging.

Brother John heaves himself into Mama Poon's yard, sort of staggers up onto her porch. Lorita comes out and helps him to a wicker chair. He sags into it heavily and sighs loudly. There he sits, arms on knees. Huge and crouching, unmoving. Eyes closed, as if asleep.

The suitcase says it all. After a little while, Lorita goes back inside. Momentarily, she reappears with a bowl of Mama Poon's hot calaloo soup.

I can smell it all the way over in our yard. Lorita sets it down before Brother John. The steam rises up toward his frowning face. He lifts the spoon to taste the soup. His eyes wide, blankly staring. He swallows. And his mouth cracks into a crooked smile.

"I know what's in that soup," I tell Johnny.

"What?"

"Oil-of-never-return."

"Gone-for-good-oil," Johnny tells me.

I nod back at him. This means obeah oil and when you eat it, you are under its power. It makes you stay with whoever it is that gives it to you.

"Him no drink it all," Johnny says hopefully.

But I see him swallow hard – every last drop.

"Him gone now, Johnny."

For a long time then we stand in the semidarkness of the croton hedge. Our eyes are on Brother John. For some reason – I don't know why – I remember how, when I was little, he used to put his hand over my face, and pretend that his huge hand was a tarantula tapping its poky way across the bridge of my nose and over my eyelids. I swear, there were times when I thought his hand *was* a spider, a real tarantula like in the song "Me see deadly black tarantula!" But afterward, as he took his hand away, I always laughed – and he did too. One sudden, loud laugh. Then it was over. The humor gone out of his eyes. Still, it was something we shared; just the two of us. The memory of this gives me a hollow feeling in the pit of my belly.

Quietly Iya comes to where we are and joins us. I feel her hand on my shoulder.

"Brother John's not coming home tonight," she says gently. Her voice is very far off, like the sea down on the reef, or the wind in the custard-apple trees in the yard.

Chapter 4

We don't talk about Brother John at supper. Iya serves the stew peas and spinners, which are skinny little dumplings, along with some bag bread and plain white rice. We eat at a table in the yard under a zinc roof. There is an outdoor fireplace for cooking. Everyone I know in Jamaica eats this way, outside under a little roof. We sit on rock-stone seats, with plates on our laps. When it gets dark, Iya lights the kerosene lantern and hangs it on a peg from one of the roofbeams.

"Where is Brother John?" Merline asks as we finish eating.

Nobody answers.

Then Maxine says, "Where him go, Iya?" Iya gets up from the table to get more lemonade. Johnny eyes me, then Bup, then Tonyskank.

All of us exchange looks. How do we tell the twins what's happened next door?

Out in the yard the standing pipe is dripping into our water bucket. It's the only sound–*pling*– you can hear.

Iya sets the lemonade pitcher on the table.

To Merline and Maxine, she says, "Brother John, him go away. We don't know when him come back, but him go away. You understand?"

The girls look at each other. They don't understand. Maybe it's just too hard for Iya to say right now.

"Brother John was in that obeah woman's yard," Merline says.

"What him do there?" Maxine asks.

"Me don't know," Iya answers.

Tonyskank gets up, excuses himself. He goes over to the standing pipe to wash his plate.

My mind wanders off somewhere, the way it does at school lots of times. I'm thinking about the crayfish in the brook way back in the bush. They're in their holes right now. My friends are gathering by the river with their bamboo torches catching them. It's cool by the river's edge. Cool and secret. I want to be there.

Iya takes the twins' plates, giving them to Johnny. Johnny bumps his head on the roof beam. He always does this. Every time.

"Bumba," Johnny mumbles, rubbing his head.

Iya catches him by the arm because he's said a bad word. "You say that again and you'll get a puppa-lick," she warns.

Johnny doesn't move. I glance at him and see that, even at thirteen, he looks like a grown man. True, he sounds like Brother John when he speaks – he's got Dadda's voice and no one else in the family has it. That deep-deep, soft-soft, husky voice. And the big head of Brother John too. Iya has a firm hold on him.

"Where you get such talk, Johnny?"

"Brother John."

Iya reluctantly lets him go. For a moment I take a good look at her as well. She always looks so neat and tidy, even in her faded house dress. Her hair is done in two braids and coiled on top of her head. Her high cheekbones and soft golden complexion are clear and beautiful, I think.

Johnny beats a retreat into the shadows to get away from her reprimand. He hates to be criticized — for anything. This is why he never liked being in school.

I turn my eyes to Bup, who is carrying his plate over to the standing pipe. Bup doesn't bump his head. He's not tall enough. Neither is Tonyskank. Neither am I.

Bup says, "Sah," to Mr. Buddy Simms, who lives on the other side of our house. That's a way of showing respect. Buddy is coming out of the bush with his string of capering goats.

Buddy's wearing his duppy-tire shoes; that is, shoes carved out of an old car tire. And he's got a pair of cutoff foot-pants, you know, halved at the knee. No matter how he dresses, though, he always looks special to us kids. It's the way he is, natural and friendly.

"Yes, sah," he says to my brothers, nodding to them. Each in turn.

It's beginning to grow dark. Shadows seem to creep out of the bush. The owl, *patoo*, flies softly out of the woods, sits on the hibiscus fence, yawning like a cat.

My brothers are fooling around in the dusk.

I'm still at the table, eating. No one ever said you had to eat fast, and I eat slower than anyone except Iya.

Then Iya calls everybody into the outdoor kitchen. I know she's going to try and straighten things out a bit. Try to answer the twins' questions about Brother John. We all sit back down on our rock-stone seats. Iya's face is hard and resigned. But I see a strength of purpose there, and her eyes appear to glow when she lights the oil lamp.

She starts off gently, so as not to scare the twins.

"I want you to listen to me, now, children. What me have to say is this. Brother John is under a spell, set up by that woman next door, that Lorita. We don't know what him going to do. All we know is what *we* must do – whether him here or not here. Brothers and sisters stick together. They don't wash away like gully water. So we have to stay together and look after one another. So it go. Whether Brother John lifts his hand to help – or not. You understand?"

No one says a word.

We nod in silence. And even though the goats are blatting in Buddy's yard, the same way they do every night at this time. Even though patoo, the owl, is making his mournful call and the peenywally fireflies are streaking past in the yard. Things are different for us.

Chapter 5

That weekend, all day Saturday and Sunday, we act as if nothing had happened. We just go about our business as usual. Once in a while, I hear Brother John laugh over in Mama Poon's yard. But I never look over there; I never want to. I don't think any of us do. It's too hurtful to think of Brother John separate from us.

On Sunday Johnny sneaks over to Mr. Nachasow's huge black mango tree. Nothing's sweeter than one of these thin-skinned mangoes. You can eat it all to, not like one of those common stringy kinds.

But the thing is, if you want to eat a black mango, you've got to be brave because Mr. Nachasow's got it in for kids who steal his fruit.

Anyway, Johnny shambles up the road, so as to cause no suspicion. Then, all of a sudden, he makes a wild run into Mr. Nachasow's yard, grabs two big mangoes, and runs off. Mr. Nachasow's right behind him, hollering like mad and running faster than a mongoose.

Johnny's laughing.

Mr. Nachasow's got a broomstick.

"Me gonna kotch you, bwai!" he yells ferociously. Johnny slips and falls. Mr. Nachasow thumps him on the back. One of the stolen mangoes rolls into the gutter. Johnny dodges another blow, gets up quick, and runs into Auntie's yard with Mr. Nachasow close behind.

Now Auntie's a good friend of all of us kids, she's everybody's auntie, no real relation but the protector of children everywhere. A tough little bantam woman – not someone to trifle with – and when stubby Mr. Nachasow stumbles into her yard, skidding to a stop, he's the one who's in trouble, not Johnny.

He's got his stick in the air, and he's all out of breath with his eyes popping out of his head. I've never seen him so angry. But Auntie, now, she's cool as a breeze and as immovable as a mountain.

Johnny sort of sidles out of the way, gets behind her, smiling wickedly.

Auntie balls up her fists.

Shes afraid of no man and Mr. Nachasow knows it.

"Yes, Mr. Nachasow?" she questions, eyebrows up, arms folded. "Morning, Auntie," he mumbles politely, taking a step back. Eyeing Johnny, he mutters something under his breath.

"Speak up, man," Auntie demands.

"Me have nuttin' fi say," Mr. Nachasow blurts out, lowering his broomstick so that it is now a walking stick.

"I got no use for foolishness, Mr. Knock-us-out!"

I laugh at this – so does Johnny whose lips are already dripping from the stolen mango, which he's eating now in full view of Mr. Nachasow. By the way, behind his back, we all call him Knock-us-out. But only Auntie dares say it to his face. And how he crumples when he hears it. Tripping over his feet to get out of there, he turns and goes up Tank Lane, defeated.

Monday morning I am awake before the first rooster. I look around the room where we boys sleep. We have two mattresses on the floor. Johnny takes up most of ours, his feet dangling off the end. Bup and Tonyskank share the other mattress.

It's a very small house, but we love it still. Growing out in the yard are lots of trees. Custard apple, soursop, mango. Iya's got gungu peas and beans all round the house too.

I can survey everything outside from the open windows inside. We have shutters, no glass. But these shutters remain open unless there's a storm.

So, right now, I hear the banana men going down the road to work. I look for Brother John, but he's not with them.

Bagga, the old man who lives at the top of the lane, comes shuffling, talking to himself. Well, he's crazy, but no one seems to mind.

Then Jerks, whose real name's Jerques. He's supposed to be the smartest guy in our class. He's always got on a long-sleeve khaki shirt, nice creased pants, and a fancy pair of Clark's desert boots. How I wish I had a pair of those!

Mister Lenny, who raises hogs, waves to me. The lane's full of frowns and smiles and all kinds of early morning people.

But no sign of Brother John.

I listen for his big, booming laugh. Don't hear anything at Mama Poon's house. Not a loose fowl, nor a little mouse. That trim tucked-up little place is so quiet. Like a dead yard, a cemetery. I wish I knew what Brother John was up to. Then I'd know better what my life was going to be like. But you never know with Brother John. He can beat you one day, praise you the next. Like most fathers, he is neither good nor bad but somewhere in between. I have to keep telling myself this. And to be patient . . . that is the hardest thing. Always I wonder what to expect. There is no telling what might happen to any of us. Mama Poon's magic seeps far and deep.

The Jonkonnu men, of whom Brother John's the leader, are now passing by. They're the most important people in Oracabessa. Every Christmas, which is just a few weeks away, all of the Jonkonnu men go upon the road, dancing and singing in front of the fancy hotels in Ocho Rios. Really, Brother John and the Jonkonnu men are famous around here, and they hold to this fame too, year-round. People look up to them because they are so good at making music and dancing and getting a crowd to go crazy with their wild gyrations.

Jonkonnu is an old African dance. Some say it used to be a way of calling up all of the old tribal powers, the gods and goddesses of the day and night, the river and bush. Nowadays it's a dance, plain and simple – but what a dance! When people see it, they remember a way of life that is gone. They remember the bad old slave days, when dancing and drumming and singing were illegal. When it was a crime to do them unless the big buckra plantation master said it was all right. Our people had tough times then – not that they're easy now, but the old days must have been really terrible.

Brother John is what you might call the Jonkonnu boss. He is not only the tallest of the tall, but the best singer and dancer of all, and, on top of that, he plays the role of the devil. There's power in that, let me tell you.

To tell the truth, we still admire and fear the devil here in Jamaica – as much as people say otherwise. Anyway, the devil's real to us. He is not just some figure of speech, or something.

Brother John plays the devil so all can see. We know the devil's always around, lurking somewhere in secret, but at Christmastime we get to see him out in the open, in all of his deviltry, his devil-may-care manner, his craziness. This is what Brother John does best – he plays at being the wickedest thing on earth.

So they come, now, this Monday morning in early December, the Jonkonnu men. Down, down the lane, they come, singing softly the way they usually do. I watch them from the open bedroom window.

There's Lucky Hill, the fireman. He's short and stocky, with a very big neck. He can blow on his bamboo fife all day long.

Next, the character they call Bosun. The name we call him is Brother Hog, and when he dances those wild jigs holding his belly and grunting like a pig, we love him so much that even now, seeing him on the road, I want to laugh. But at Jonkonnu, when he wears his sailor's suit and his eerie mask made out of a cigar box painted red, black, and white, he's scary too.

Then there's Clappy, the graterman, who plays the washboard grater. He puts thimbles on his fingers and scratches the washboard in time to the fife and drum. Clappy doesn't wear any special costume when he's performing, but he's skinny and his bony dancing also makes me crack up.

Now comes Red, the man who plays the part of a royal person. We call him Crown in the Jonkonnu dance, and he dresses like a king in plaid clothes with a mesh mask of many colors. He's strange looking. But Red's just Red the rest of the year, a man whose high-color skin has a coppery cast.

My favorite of the Jonkonnu men is Sticky, the drummer. I see him walking slow and easy just now. He waves and I wave back. Everyone likes Sticky because he's so good-natured and it's hard to provoke him or make him angry. There's something else about him too. He stands a little apart from the rest, sort of by himself. His real work away from the docks and the bananas is at Golden head Beach Hotel where he manages the skiffs.

Sticky's always been my friend. He takes time to talk to me and he listens to what I say. No other grown-up except Buddy Simms does this – listens to me and thinks about what I am telling him.

I watch the Jonkonnu men go down Tank Lane, singing their song, the one that goes, "Day-oh, daylight come an me wan go home, day-oh, is a day-ay-ay-o."

The voices are mellow in the morning air. The sun lights the flame-heart tree on the hill, making it seem to burn.

Well, I am looking everywhere, but I don't see Brother John anywhere. I glance at Mama Poon's house for the first time in two days. It's all shuttered up, as if no one's living there.

Chapter 6

Thinking about Jonkonnu and Brother John reminds me that Christmas is just three weeks away. I wonder how we're going to make enough money to put food on the table, plus have something left over for the holiday.

Mama Poon's house is all shuttered up. There'll be no money coming from there, no charity, that's for sure. Now that *she's* got him — and we *don't* — whatever money he makes at the docks is going to be *hers*, and hers alone. Not that it was much easier before this happened. Thinking back, I can't remember a single time when we ever had any *extra anything*. Life with Brother John has always been a chancy-dancy business, with him always skipping out and Iya always picking up the slack. Maybe that's the way it is with all families, I don't know. All I know for sure is that being poor means being hungry, and even when you're full, you're thinking about the next meal and the one after that.

I am thinking about that oil-of-never-return. It must've really knocked Brother John out. He'd sooner die than miss "a work," and yet that's just what he's doing by sleeping the morning away.

Iya interrupts my daydreaming.

"Tall T, you have work to do. Get off that bed and carry-come my breakfast water." Johnny rolls on to his back, yawning.

"Yes, Iya," I say. I tug on my threadbare khaki pants and my hand-me-down short-sleeve shirt with the two buttons in front. My pants zipper starts to slide down as soon as I get it zipped. Oh, pretty soon it'll be as wide as a church door and I've got to keep a watchful eye on it all the time or I'll embarrass myself at school.

Tonyskank and Bup are up now and getting into their school uniforms. Their clothes aren't shabby like mine. Theirs are newer. Mine are just the luck of the draw. When Johnny outgrows something, then I get it. And let me tell you, Johnny wears clothes hard.

Shoes . . . another thing I don't have. Tonyskank and Bup don't have them either, or the twins, and especially not Johnny, as he's not even going to school anymore since he quit last year to earn some money for the family. He does just about anything too. Sells carved coconut birds, shows people the best places to swim down at the beach. He makes a little money doing these things every day – not much money, unfortunately. But whatever it is, he shares it with all of us, so no one feels left out.

I fill two water pails at the standing pipe and carry them to where Iya is cooking cornmeal porridge over the fire. It takes four pails each morning to do the cooking and washing.

Some parrots shriek in the pawpaw trees. We sit down on our rock stones to eat. I help serve the twins their porridge. Iya serves Johnny and Bup.

"You boys are old enough to earn this family's keep," she says between servings. I watch her drinking her morning tea of bitter cerasee. "We just have to make a plan."

I am starting on my porridge when Iya says in the low, soft voice she uses when speaking about matters of faith and family, "We can make do. We have to." She winces at her tea cup. Cerasee is *so* bitter. In Jamaica most people drink it for nine mornings, then quit for a time. It's supposed to clean you inside, but I think it's terrible stuff.

"So how we gonna get by without Brother John?" Tonyskank asks, licking his porridge spoon.

"Me sell the nice conch shells to tourists," Johnny replies. "One good big shell worth a whole day's food for this family." He is eating his breadfruit like a piece of toasted bread. Idly, he watches Buddy Simms lead his goats back out to pasture. Looking at Johnny, as if for the first time, I realize it's Johnny and not me who favors Brother John. Also, that "rough-tough" voice that sounds like the sea.

"We know you help, Johnny," Iya says with confidence. "She continues, "I'm going to do more laundry for the tourists at Goldenhead Beach Hotel. I'm going to clean the house of Mrs.Scott. We'll manage, somehow."

"Me have to quit school?" I ask.

I don't want to do that because I like school. I'm good at it. But if I have to quit, I will.

Mama's face tightens with the mention of me quitting. "You won't do any such thing. It's bad enough Johnny's out of school. No, Tall T, you've got to stay in."

She pauses, sighs, rubs her palms against her dress. "But you must work too."

Johnny gives a husky laugh, polishes off his breadfruit.

I say, "There's lots of things I can do, Iya. Don't worry. Johnny and I can carve coconut birds and sell them. We can boil up some coconut oil and sell that for suntan oil down at the beach. We can always sell peanuts down there too."

"You could make as much money as Brother John," Merline offers. She is finishing her porridge, setting down her spoon. I look at her neatly dressed in her best school clothes. To see the twins, you'd never know we were hard-pressed. Neat little blue jumpers, pleated and nice. White shirts, starched with cassava juice and hot-ironed by Iya. Merline and Maxine look good, they really do.

I gaze at Bup and Tonyskank. For all their grown-up talk, they're a couple of *pickneys*, as they say. They've never worked, never been asked to.

"Can I work?" Bup questions. "I'm nine now."

"I know how old you are." Iya chuckles.

"And me?" Tonyskank asks.

"I know your age," she replies, smiling.

"No, I mean, can I work too?"

Iya shakes her head as she sips the cerasee tea. "You two will have the job of looking out for the twins."

Bup and Tonyskank frown.

Well, I know I'm the one who will shoulder the load. Iya's always counted on me for that. She knows it, I know it, and the others know it too. Families are like that – there's always one member who's expected to do more than anyone else. It's not that I'm better than Johnny, but I've always been there when Iya needed me. Even more than Brother John ... when he still lived with us. I'm used to this. In fact, I like it. I like being the one people depend on.

So, even if Iya doesn't say anything this morning about what I'm *supposed* to do, I know what she *expects* me to do. She wants me to figure something out that will get us past this difficult time.

And I will.

I must.

Chapter 7

The problem is, how do I go to school, do my homework, and earn money all at the same time?

Johnny's thinking the same thing that I am. "How is Tall T going to go to school and make money too?" he asks Iya. She looks at me knowingly.

"He will have to be like Jacob in the Bible. Jacob who dreamed, who made good things happen because he was a dreamer."

Tonyskank's eyes are crinkling. He remembers the old story that Iya has read to us so many times. "Jacob," he says, "was a dreamer all right." Then he adds with amusement, "Who beat up his brother."

"His brother was good-for-nothing," Bup scoffs, pushing at Tonyskank. Iya puts down her teacup. I stack the empty porridge bowls. Then I give them to Tonyskank and Bup, who carry them out to the standing pipe and wash them clean.

Iya says to all of us, "Remember, children, Jacob wasn't just a dreamer, you know. He was a seer. He saw the angels climbing up and down on the ladder to heaven."

Is that the same Jacob Ladder going down to the dock?" Merline asks.

I chuckle at that.

"It's the same, in spirit, child," Iya explains softly. Merline says, I know." In my mind, just now, I see Brother John's long, muscular arms ascending the Ladder, drawing his great body up the cliff, and out of the fig leaves that seem to drown all but his head. It takes strength to climb the Ladder because it's more than fifty feet from top to bottom. It takes great willpower. You get tired of pulling yourself up with your arms. Maybe the angels could float, but men have to work to draw their bodies aloft. Most of the banana men go around on the road, which takes longer, but it's not so much toil and trouble.

I think about it this way: if I could climb the Ladder the way Brother John does, I would be a man. And, like Jacob, maybe I could see halfway to heaven too.

I think Iya knows that I will take Jacob's part. He was a *dreamer,* but also a *leader.* He was the younger brother who was favored over the older brother in the end. But how am I to be so favored? How am I to prove myself as a leader? I wish I might climb the Jacob Ladder, a wish is a wish. My arms aren't strong enough. If I fell trying to make the climb, I believe I would die on the rocks below.

Tony Skank comes back with the clean, stacked bowls. For some reason, as I look upon him now, I think that he is the most proper of the brothers. His feet, even bare, draw no attention. It's that way with him. Neat as a pin, never messy.

Going to school, you can get away without wearing shoes. However, if you don't have a uniform – khaki shirt and khaki pants – you can't go to school at all. And, if your uniform's untidy, you might be told to go home. That's a new rule – as of last Friday– that Iya doesn't even know about.

She doesn't know, and I won't tell her, that my clothes are unpresentable. Why should I worry her with one more little thing? Doesn't she have enough on her mind?

But what if I'm sent home on account of my worn-out shirt and my threadbare pants? Well, I guess that would solve one problem, anyway.

"Isn't Brother John going to help out?" Tonyskank asks.

"At Jonkonnu time, his heart will have to melt. It have to," Iya replies.

"He'll have money," I put in. "People always pitch money at the Jonkonnu dancers."

"Gambling money that," Johnny mutters gruffly, shaking his head. Suddenly, we hear a loud noise coming from Mama Poon's yard.

All of us look over the croton hedge and see Brother John, fumbling with his clothes, trying to get dressed. He's out in the yard in his underwear, and, while he is pulling on his clothes, Mama Poon's berating him. Lorita's eating a piece of papaya, smiling.

I've never seen Brother John look so small. He seems to be shrinking under the spell of Mama Poon, getting littler by the moment.

Iya says sharply, "That's no concern of ours – what goes on in that yard, children. Go to school now."

Then to me, "Tall T, check Brother John at lunch. He must give you children some money to eat. Even he has a heart somewhere in that big chest of his."

I nod. I have a feeling he will give us the slip, as he has before. If he does, there'll be no money until Iya gets paid for doing laundry at the end of the week. Anyway, we shuffle out through the gate. I take a quick peek over my shoulder. Mama Poon is towering over Brother John. She stands, arms folded, head covered by a red scarf.

Brother John, that big, serious, strong-arm man dressing in the yard.

Clicking shut the front gate, I feel a whole lot of heads turning. The whole neighborhood. Listening, watching. Their eyes eating us alive as we go down Tank Lane to Oracabessa Primary School.

Chapter 8

At the school yard, Tonyskank goes his way, Bup goes his, and the twins go theirs. I'm standing by myself, wondering what I'm going to do.

Iya says I'm supposed to go to school, but I've got to earn money too. My mind, right now, is on the money, not the school. Without money, there'll be no school for me. Nor for the others as well. In Jamaica you've got to pay for books, uniforms, tuitions – everything. If you're too poor to pay for these things, you can't go to school.

Many is the time, I know, that Iya has gone without food for herself, so that we children could stay in school. And, all the while, Brother John was earning big wages and throwing them away by gambling at the docks.

Now, what am I to do?

If I can find Brother John, maybe I can wheedle a few dollars from him.

As I am standing there, in the school yard, trying to adjust my broken zipper, painfully aware of my bare feet, this boy named Belling comes up to me.

Belling's not too good at schoolwork, but teachers like him anyway, and he loves being at school. It's everything to him, his whole life. Nobody can ring the school bell like Belling, which is how he got that nickname. One thing for sure — he can really make that bronze bell ring.

Normally, Belling's barefoot. Like me. But this morning he's got on a pair of polished leather shoes.

"Where'd you get *those*?" I ask.

"Uncle." He grins.

I grin back, but my smile fades.

"I got my uniform from my cousin," he says cheerfully. Uneasily, I regard his well-pressed khakis. His clothes are mostly as worn-out as mine. But today he's got these tailor-made trousers and shirt. He hardly looks like Belling anymore. I check to see that my shirt is hanging over my broken zipper.

How many times had Brother John promised to buy me a proper uniform? How many times had he sworn he'd buy me a pair of leather shoes?

I remember once when he was barbering the whole neighborhood (another of his jobs) and I had to wait my turn, which was most of Sunday, I remember. But when my turn came under the ackee tree, he put his big hand over my face and laughed. And I laughed too. Funny, how things come back when you least expect them to. That huge smothering hand over my face before he got busy trimming my hair. It was his little joke *with me*, not something he shared with anyone else. With my brothers and sisters, he just got busy and gave them their haircut. No joking business – but with me, it was different. I smile, even now, at the memory of his hand that was larger than my face.

Now Belling's standing in front of me, with his melon-shaped head and his pockmarked cheeks, and his sporty dress-up shoes. There he is, clanging the commencement bell and smirking at me and my bare feet and my broken zipper.

Mrs. Hellen, the principal, sees me and walks over to us.

"You know the rule," she says coldly.

I say nothing.

"Uton, I said on Friday *every* student must follow the rule. We have a strict dress code now."

"Me know the rule," I say.

Out of the corner of my eye I see the twins.

They wave at me. I don't wave back. I can't. Not while Mrs. Hellen is staring at me. I step back a little.

Mrs. Hellen wearing her spotless dark blue blouse and jacket snaps at me, "Tell Brother John I want to talk to him." Then abruptly she strides into the cool stone schoolhouse, with Jerks right beside her. His Clark's desert boots looking so fine, his self-important smile shining like the sun.

"Tomorrow, Uton," Belling mimics, "proper shoes and proper uniform – *or else!*"

I stand there staring at the guinep tree in the empty dusty school yard. I watch Belling pull the bell rope. He loves this job, which is his whole identity. Take it away from Belling and ... who knows what would happen?

Well, I say let Belling have his new shoes and let him have his precious bell rope. Let him.

We always say, when it comes somebody's turn to get something, "Your time a-come." Which means, everybody gets a little luck sometime.

Looking down at my feet covered with white talcum dust, I wonder if my turn is coming. Will I have one at all?

Chapter 9

As the last student enters Oracabessa Primary School, I make my move. I go out upon the street, away from the school yard, away from the echoes of Belling's bell.

Iya won't have to know – yet.

The streets of Oracabessa are hot. Even on a December morning like this one, the sun is strong and bright. I'm not going anywhere, in particular. I am just walking, for, as they say, "Walk for nothing, better than sit down for nothing."

From the hill that overlooks the dock, I see the banana men and hear them too.

They're singing an old toting song.

Poor mon tum out, but de money no dere
Beg hard by excuse, but de money no dere
Go clear a foreign, but de money no dere
Work all day a dock, and de money come dere.

I look down the long row of shining backs and shining arms, but when I hear the singing, I don't think of anyone working. The song is part of the work, a reason for why it gets done. Yet those voices, rising in the risen sun, do most of the work, I think.

Out in the harbor, the British freighter, *The Producer*, with its huge cranes hanging over the deck, lies upon a glittery blue sea. Already, the tote boats are taking the great bunches of green bananas out to *The Producer*.

Brother John, the most formidable rower of all, is hauling the largest load. His boat is low in the water from the great weight of so many banana bunches. Somehow, I can see Johnny with his long arms and big shoulders – doing that same work, but not me. I'd love to go on *The Producer*, just to feel the deck under my feet, and to explore all around it. But I have no desire to tote bananas under the cruel sun. That's not for me.

Above and behind me, the poinciana trees flash their long pods, which rattle in the wind. Some little boys are playing with one of the pods in front of the Oracabessa Public Library.

Shk-shk-shk, the poincianas rattle. They're rattling in time to the singing banana men, these little children with dry poinciana pods in their hands. I wish I were in time *with* something, *for* something. I wish I were going *somewhere, anywhere*. Not just out walking to kill time.

Then I look at the library. Just up the street from the Jacob Ladder. If I went there, who'd notice? Who'd care? The library looks cool, inviting.

So I go inside where it is nice, with the sea breeze coming off the headland hill. I step into the library's single room and, trying to look natural, I sit down at a handmade cedar table.

Immediately, the librarian, Miss Patterson, speaks to me. She is a light-skinned woman with large full eyes, set behind black-rimmed, square eyeglasses. She wears her black hair straightened, and very neat, so that it glows. Like Mrs. Hellen, Miss Patterson looks official in her prim jacket and skirt, her stockings and heels. Those heels go *pong, pong* on the hard pine floor.

Tall T, why aren't you in school, mon?" Miss Patterson is wiping a book with a dry cloth. I tuck my dusty bare feet under the table and clear my throat.

"Me don't have to go to school today," I reply as casually as I can.

She sniffs, shakes her head.

Miss Patterson isn't anyone you can fool. Soft and sweet, she is also as tight as a broom. Her purpose is always to sweep foolishness out of her way.

"You think me *blind*?" She laughs.

I shake my head. "No, Miss Patterson."

"Tall T, you think me blind as a rat bat?"

Please, I pray silently, *don't kick me out of here, Miss Patterson. Me have nowhere to go.*

She stares at me, as if she can almost hear me praying. Her intent eyes seem to soften.

I try to plead my case.

"Miss Patterson. You know the new rule? No proper uniform, no school. Well, me don't have them thing. So, me can't go to school right now. Now, if me go home, me get a *mumma-lick*. If me go to the dock, me get a *puppa-lick*. So, let me ask you, where am I to go?"

Miss Patterson's eyes seem to take this in. Her expression is thoughtful, slightly puzzled too.

"Please," I beg, "don't kick me out of here just now."

When I say this – not thinking of doing anything but telling the truth – even if it should get me kicked out, I feel that Miss Patterson has taken up my problem almost as if it were her own.

She says gently, "You want to read, Tall T? You want to learn about good men and bad men and all kind of in-between men? You want to stretch your mind along with those tall, tall legs of yours?"

I nod, *yes*, I do.

Miss Patterson steps, *pong-pong-pong,* over to where I am sitting. Then she eases her ample, rose-scented body close to mine. Resting her elbow on the table, she asks me a confidential question.

"Are you free, Tall T?"

"What you mean *free*?"

"Just so."

"*What*, just so?"

"Me ask you a library question. In school you get school question. True?"

I nod.

"Here, you get library question."

What is she getting at?

"You mean free like a bird?" I ask. "Or free like a boy trapped between the devil and the deep blue sea?" That just spills out of my mouth. I didn't *plan* to say it, I *said* it.

She grins warmly at me. "Eh-eh, so your head not just a hat rack."

Encouraged, I continue, "Me no free, Miss Patterson. If me would be free, me would be inna school, or working – somewhere. Maybe down at the docks."

"*What?*" she teases, drawing a breath. "*You* could tote a bunch of banana like the big men down there?" Her spectacled eyes close as she shakes her head, and chuckles.

"Yes, Miss Patterson."

All right, boy," she says, "tote *this* now!"

Then she lifts an enormous Bible from off of one of the shelves, and passes it to me. The book's so heavy, I almost drop it on my bare foot.

"Flip it open – and *read!*" she commands.

Pong, pong, she goes back to her desk. I hear her singing softly, "*De bwai tote de banana, oh.*" She's making fun of me, but not with malice. It's funny, really. How could a boy carry a hundred pound banana bunch on his back, or throw it from one man to another all day long? Or climb the Jacob Ladder?

"Remember," she reminds, "no man is free who can't read the holy Scripture."

I nod my head and begin to read.

I am in library school now.

Chapter 10

My fingers run along the gold-edged pages of the huge black leather Bible. The gilt dust from the crisp lacquered paper comes off on my hand like the powder of a butterfly's wing. Admiring it for a moment, I leaf some more, stopping, by accident, at Genesis 28:16.

And Jacob awaked out of his sleep, and he said, Surely the Lord is in this place; and I knew it not.

I think about this for the longest time. Here Jacob was waking after his dream of the angels climbing up and down the ladder to heaven. He knew for the first time that the ground he slept on was holy. He understood that the ladder was real, as were the angels. And that the Lord was above blessing all things below. Blessing the earth on which he slept.

I wonder if God knows that I, Tall T, am here in the Oracabessa Public Library? Does He know that I am but a few steps from the Jacob Ladder? Is our Jamaican ground blessed too? Is the Lord here too? And am I like Jacob ... and know it not?

As I am thinking these thoughts, the words begin to wobble on the page. They waver and my head swims. Like Jacob, I blink myself awake.

Outside in the sun the poinciana pods rustle on the tin roof.

In the light of midmorning, the song of the banana men climbs the hand-carved stairs of the Jacob Ladder, filtering through the library and entering the seashell of my ear. I think of how my father and his friends climb the Ladder with careworn hands, and how they are the grandchildren of African slaves, but if the Bible speaks the truth, we are blessed and the ground we live on is holy.

The song of the banana men rises and falls in the leaf-flickering light.

Praise God and me big right hand
Me live and die a banana man.

I look closely at my arm — what a puny little bicep
I have!

Will I grow to be as strong as Brother John?

I think not. But I can still dream ... like Jacob.

Outside the honk of a Morris motorcar in the
sunstruck street. The whistle of a peanut vendor piping
high and away, carrying me along with it down the
narrow street toward Port Maria.

My eyelids grow heavy. My head droops. Again I
drift off.

Then a hard hand clamps on my shoulder.

"None of that puss-nap business," a voice reproves.

I snap awake. Miss Patterson.

"Time for lunch, Tall T," she reminds. "Get some
fresh air and some food in your belly now."

I hasten out into the buttery sunlight. On the street,
I run into Tonyskank, Bup, and the twins. They
imagine I've skipped school in order to get some lunch
money from Brother John.

I shrug when I see them.

"Brother John up the Ladder yet?" Bup asks.

"Me no know."

They look at me, as if I could control this event.

"Me don't see Brother John," Bup says.

Tonyskank crinkles his eyes. "Mek we find him."

We walk toward the Jacob Ladder. On the hot, bright road, running south of the carved stairs, there are patty places, rum shops, and alongside the road, little cooking fires where food is being prepared for the banana men.

The air's full of the smell of bubbling coconut oil and charcoal fires. I smell pan breads and dumplings cooking and roasting breadfruit. Fried chicken and fish, and the delectable smell of bammy.

The five of us turn our heads away from these enticing odors. We walk to the edge of the Ladder and look way deep into the murmuring green fig leaves. The banana men, leaving the dock for lunch, are splintering up into groups.

One by one, a few strong men pull themselves up the stairs of the great Ladder. I wonder at their strength. Their muscular forearms bulge and shine with sweat. I ask myself, once again, if I could climb such a great height using my arms.

Then, peering through the lime green leaves, I spot Brother John. He's down there in the blue shadow, getting ready to come up. His shirt's wide open, his broad chest bright and wet. He's right at the base of the Ladder. I know he's borrowed some money from one of his friends. That's what he always does after he gambles and loses on Friday nights.

I watch his huge fist dip into his trouser pocket. Then his hand shoots out, clasping his buddy Bosun by the shoulder. The two of them laugh.

"I'm going down the road to meet him," Merline shouts.

Maxine hangs back, unsure. She looks at me hurriedly, her face all worried. "You stay with me, Tall T?"

"Me stay all the while."

Merline runs into the white sunlight down the chalk dust, marl road. Bup whispers, "Don't she know him come up the Ladder?"

"Sometime," says Tonyskank, "him go on the road instead."

All of us are intent upon watching Brother John, who is just standing there at the bottom of the Ladder talking with Bosun. We don't know which way he'll take, but if he goes out to the road, Merline will meet him. If he comes up the Ladder, we'll catch him for sure.

"Brother John soon come," I tell them.

But when I look down along the cool, dappled shade of the cliff through which the banana men move ever upward, Brother John is suddenly missing.

I can't believe it. In a second, *he's given us the slip.*

He has vanished into thin air.

I squint into the distance – and see him over by the cove. There is a goat path there, one that leads to Oracabessa going the back way.

Why didn't I think of this?

In the blink of an eye, he's gone again.

Defeated, I walk down the hill to fetch Merline. When we return the boys have gone away. They'll find friends and food. Or else, they'll get some fruit that hangs over someone's fence. It's not wrong to take fruit, if it's on the street side of the fence. If you take it from the owner's side, it's called *praedial larceny*. I know that because we studied it in school.

For the next few minutes the banana men hoist themselves up the Ladder, their feet sort of dancing on the clay stairs, as they rise up into the shade of the fig trees that grow along the cliff.

Old Mr. Lenny appears; I greet him. His serious face breaks into a smile. He says, "Tall T," and nods, then heads over to Mr. Hopson's Lunch Shop.

Merline and Maxine stand next to me, waiting for me to do something. On the grassy knoll where we're perched, you can see the blue of the sea.

The twins are standing so pretty, so hopeful, holding hands.

Sticky, the drummer, comes along the road and I ask him if he's seen Brother John anywhere. Wiping his face with a handkerchief, he shakes his head. Then he puts a hand on my shoulder and gives me a little pat. I watch him walk to Mr. Hopson's to get a bun-and-cheese. Halfway over there, crossing the road, he pauses and asks Mr. Lenny, "Brother John, where him go?" Mr. Lenny shrugs from the cool darkness of the shop where he is munching a meat patty.

Sticky walks back to me. "Need some money, Tall T?"

If it were just me, I wouldn't ask. But it's for the twins.

"Me owe Brother John, mon." Sticky grins crookedly in the sun's glare, his beard shining with beads of sweat. He presses a handful of dollars into my hand. "That's too much," I protest.

Sticky explains, "One week ago me lose bad at the bone dice." He sighs and rolls his eyes. "Brother John bail me out. So, now, me bail you. No problem, Tall T."

I know, however, that Sticky is the one man in Oracabessa who *never* gambles. Suddenly, I wish *he* was my father. And I think he feels as warmly toward me as I do for him.

At Mr. Hopson's I order the twins and me a bun-and-cheese and soft drinks, plus three peppermint candies. There's still enough left over for my brothers, and for the rest of the week. I'm so relieved that I want to cry. But after eating, I go back to the library, somehow tired and dispirited. In spite of Sticky's kindness, I feel depressed. Is *this* how begging makes you feel?

Chapter 11

We struggle through the week to get to Friday, which is payday for Brother John. However, before I can squeeze him for a little money, he gambles it away again. I am not quick enough when it comes to Brother John.

Sticky's loan kept us going all week long. At last, Saturday comes and with it Johnny's money. He's been selling picture frames, conch shells, and peanuts down at Goldenhead Beach Hotel. One day he overheard a lady at the beach say she wished she could iron her clothes, and he told her, "Me mumma can do that." And Iya does, and we make some more money.

Buddy Simms gets me part-time work as a carpenter's helper. Mr. Hopson gives me a little delivery work, so I am able to make a contribution to the family earnings. Saturday night I give Iya all that I've made — almost twenty dollars. Johnny's money comes to more. Iya looks at all the crumpled bills and presses them flat with her palms. She looks as if she's going to cry. She doesn't, though. She just flattens the money on the table and counts it under the glow of the kerosene lantern in our outside kitchen.

She sighs. "This will *just* cover the rent. It's a good start."

I know there are so many more things – school tuition, shoes, uniforms, Christmas.

She presses the dollar bills, as if for emphasis. Then she tells us what Buddy Simms' wife told her.

"I don't want to scare you, children. I just want you to know because if worse comes to worse, there is always another way we can make do."

"What is it, Iya?" Johnny says hoarsely while chewing on a piece of jackfruit, the stickiest, candiest-tasting fruit in all Jamaica. The twins share it with him, careful not to get any of the juice on their dresses. Iya looks tired as she tells us, "Mrs. Simms say, 'all dem children dem can go to a relation *fi* stay!'"

"What you tell her, Iya?" I ask.

"I tell her I wouldn't send you children away for anything in the world. That's what *my* mama did when I was little – sent us away when the family was so poor. I tell her no matter what, no matter how broke, I can't send my children off to any relative."

Bup says, "Iya, if you had to, I mean *had* to, where *would* you send us?"

"And, *who* would you send?" Tonyskank asks.

Iya frowns. Her eyes dart off into the night, then come back to us.

"I would send the twins, I suppose, to St. Elizabeth ... to stay with my relations."

I glance at Merline. She doesn't flinch. Neither does Maxine.

"If that be so, that be so," Merline says in such a grown-up voice, I can hardly believe that she's said it. Maxine nods, in perfect accord.

"Don't you worry, Iya," Johnny says soothingly. His voice is sandpaper on a rough plank.

A moth, the kind we call bat, flies into our midst with a summery flutter.

Bup swings at it with his hand, misses. He hits Tonyskank and the two start a little sparring match in the grass. We all begin to laugh.

I guess that's when I know, somehow, that everything's going to be all right.

As long as we can laugh.

Chapter 12

Monday, like always, I skip school. I go to the library where Miss Patterson has a book for me – a clothbound collection of stories about our national heroes. I've been reading western novels, mysteries, and adventures. I'm surprised at how fast I can read when I want to. So is Miss Patterson. But this morning, she wants me to read something else.

"If you are in library school, you have to read what's on the list." She smiles.

"The *list? What* list, Miss Patterson?"

Her round wide eyes regard me. She is wearing dark red lipstick and her thin lips are tight. She explains. "The list is anything I devise for your edification, Tall T. Understood?"

"Yes, Miss Patterson." She places the book in my hands. I hold it, but my eyes rove across the shelves to the place where *The Gleaner*, Jamaica's daily newspaper is hung out on a wooden scroll. Headline reads: **Man In Bush Chops Two**. I want to know more about that, but the heavy book, now resting on my lap, is on the list, so I'll have to wait until later to find out about the bush-chopping man.

The thing is, I've discovered something. In words, things happen. Truths are revealed. Life, *itself,* is words.

I never knew that. I certainly never learned it in school. Now, I read everything I can put my hands on – even matchboxes. For Miss Patterson, I accept the assignment of national heroes and start reading about them.

I read the chapter about Tacky, the seventeenth-century slave leader from the parish of St. Mary. This was the man who jumped 150 feet off a waterfall rather than submit to slavery. It's said that he died at the bottom of Tacky Falls, and people, to this day, have seen his spirit.

My favorite hero, though, is Nanny. It was she who walked from Moore Town in Portland all the way across the John Crow Mountains and the Blue Mountains to the secret hiding place of that other great runaway slave leader, Cudjoe. Nanny and Cudjoe were called *maroons*, which in Spanish means runaways. But they were really Ashanti warriors from the Gold Coast of Africa.

Nanny and Cudjoe beat the British and secured land for their people under their own sovereign flag, and it is still that way today. Then I come to the part where Nanny actually caught bullets with her buttocks!

Just then Miss Patterson touches me on the shoulder, and I jump up into the air. She exclaims, "How you read, Tall T as if you were really there!"

And I say, "*I was*, Miss Patterson, I *really was*."

I didn't know that you could meet such people in the quiet stillness of the library. I didn't know you could kind of talk to them, ask them questions, and read their answers. All these things I didn't know.

It makes me feel a lot less scared about my own life, our own lives. You know, Iya has always said to us, "If you bring food into the house, know that you will share it with your brothers and sisters. If you have a piece of *bulla bread,* know that you will cut it into six pieces. He who eats food all for himself and doesn't share, eats alone."

I'm not surprised, therefore, when I find out that Nanny lived the same way. Cudjoe, the same.

Whatever they *had*, they *shared*. And that was how, I discover, the British were unable to defeat them as a people.

As I walk home this Friday, I hear the voices of heroes ringing in my ears, and I don't even hear Belling, passing me on the street, when he says, "Hey, Library Boy, when you going to get your uniform?"

What does it matter if people look at me funny? At night, while we're eating supper, we hear Brother John next door, talking to Mama Poon and Lorita. His rumbly voice is soft and affectionate in the folding dusk. Once, I imagine I see a tear in Iya's eye. But she turns away so fast, I'm not sure it was really there.

That tear is always there, though. It's in each of our hearts whether we hear his voice or not. Whether we wait for him at the top of the Jacob Ladder, or whether

58

we see him coming up Tank Lane at day's end. There's a Brother John tear in each of us, each one of us.

But no one can see it.

Chapter 13

All that weekend Johnny and I earn money.

First, we go down to the beach to try and sell some carved coconut birds to the tourists there. However, we find out Saturday morning that there's a new beach rule. You can't sell anything to tourists unless they ask to buy something first. Since vendors aren't allowed on the beach, this is a tough rule.

How do you *sell* someone something when you can't *talk* to them?

Well, the rule doesn't say you can't wave to people.

So, Johnny and I hide behind a big rock on the beach. We wave at the people on the sand by the sea.

Sometimes, they wave back.

Mostly they don't.

One time this man sees us, and he really gives us a real sweep of the hand. Then he comes closer, still waving. We beckon to him, but we keep ourselves low, and almost out of sight, with just our hands sticking up. The man strides up to our hiding place.

"What are you boys doing?"

He seems friendly.

"My name's Bernard," he says warmly, putting out his hand. We greet him, shaking hands all around.

"What's *that*?" he asks. He points at the coconut bird Johnny's holding in his hand.

"Coconut bird," Johnny says huskily.

"Well, well. That's made real nice," the man remarks. "Would you sell it to me?"

Johnny grins, ear to ear. His grin's even bigger than his voice.

The friendly man smiles broadly. Then all three of us start laughing.

After which he offers us a five-dollar bill. Johnny accepts it and he puts the coconut bird into the man's hands.

"By the way," Bernard says, "if you make more of these, I will take them back home to Canada with me. The hospital where I work could really use these to decorate the windows."

So all that day and Sunday, Johnny and I carve the little birds for Bernard. We also make picture frames, bracelets made out of bent forks, and a Canadian coat of arms that I look up in the encyclopedia at the library.

Well, it's the coat of arms that is the hit with Bernard. On Monday morning we show him all the stuff we've made and his appraising eye gets stuck on that coat of arms.

"What's *this*?" he asks. "Is it what I think it is?"

I say, "That's your coat of arms."

He shakes his head and smiles. He keeps turning it around and around in his hands, smiling all the while.

"You boys are *geniuses*," he exclaims, clapping Johnny and me on the back.

After he pays us for everything we've made, he gives us the first fifty-dollar bill we've ever seen. Then Bernard orders twenty more coats of arms.

"How long are you staying here at Goldenhead?" I ask him.

"Until the middle of next week. Think you can do it by then?"

Johnny says sure before I can even give it some thought and, afterward, as we head home, I feel my steps lighten.

Another good thing happens that same day. Mama Poon shows me some kindness. I am near her yard peering over the croton bushes looking for Brother John. Usually she chases me away, but today she opens the door and puts a crocus bag at the top step of the porch. "Come, bwai," she calls, and goes inside.

I remain by the crotons, unsure, unmoving. I am like Nanny, standing before the oppressor. Unflinching, I stare back at her as she looks at me through the window. Then she bursts out laughing.

"*Likkle* Breddeh John," she chuckles.

I walk up and take the bag. Then I walk back to the croton fence. "What you fussin' round here for?" she snaps.

I look directly into her eyes. She roars with laughter.

"Ah, how the bwai do grow to be a mon," she remarks. And then she says, "You the one. You the one fi true."

"*What one?*"

"One that favor Brother John."

I nod stiffly but proudly. Though I can't explain why I'm feeling proud, I do feel it.

She looks me up and down.

I look her over. She smiles ... almost warmly, I think. I feel prickly under my shirt. I think of the saying: *your best friend could be your worst enemy.* But I turn it around: *your worst enemy could be your best friend.*

Going back into her house, I hear Mama Poon mumble, "Man enough to look me in the eye, old enough to carry yam out of me yard." By which she means that if I can face her, I am fit to carry off a bag of yams, which I do, while she's back there on her porch smoking and laughing to herself.

After this, each week there is a bag of what we call *food* – yam, potato, cassava – on the porch. This is the real yard food we live on, what we use to quell the *white squall* in the belly.

Iya doesn't ask where the bags come from; nor does anyone else.

They know.

And, shortly after that, the week before Christmas, Brother John meets me at the top of the Jacob Ladder.

He seems to see me for the first time. In all this time of working and reading and struggling and praying he hasn't really taken stock of me, nor I, really, of him.

He eyes me critically.

"You bigger," he says. He is unsmiling. I watch him wipe the sweat from his forehead with a handkerchief.

"Yes, mon. Me grow."

Brother John smiles once, hard and fast.

"You want to be the devil's treasurer, bwai? Carry me purse at Jonkonnu, one week from now?"

I hear myself say, "Yes."

Can it be true? Has Brother John *really* asked me to hold the money-purse for the Jonkonnu dancers as they dance about town? That's a job for a grown man. Why is he asking *me*, a mere boy? I hear him say, in my head, *You bigger.* I hear that, over and over.

And so now I am the devil's treasurer.

Chapter 14

The last day of school before the holidays is Thursday. On this day, I walk with my brothers and sisters to the school yard. There's Belling, swinging his bell rope, as usual. But his shoes are scuffed, dirty looking. His eyes are on me as he pulls the rope. One arm is raised above the other, as if he is going up to heaven. I know that he knows what everyone knows in Oracabessa. In two days in our town the news is out.

Everyone knows that I am the devil's treasurer.

People seem to be seeing me differently. Even Belling, the great bell swinger, has a little hidden envy in his eyes. Well, it's the same look I gave him – some weeks before – when I first saw his shiny new shoes. Jerks too. His thin, wary eyes studying me for the first time.

As I leave my brothers and sisters at the school yard and walk slowly uphill to the library, I am lost in thought. Thinking about my good luck, and Brother John's kindness. My appointment. And Christmas coming.

Today is the eighteenth of December. That means all this week the Jonkonnu men will be doing their rehearsals for the great event. Although there's no set rule for this, Jonkonnu usually comes on Christmas Day. Now I am thinking that maybe this year we will have a fancy Christmas after all. I mean with the extra money I'm going to earn with Brother John, there will certainly be some special food and trimmings on Christmas Day.

You see, the people always reward the Jonkonnu men with plenty of coin. My job will be to pick it up and put it in the purse. Later, when the earnings are divided up equally, I'll get my share too. Who knows – it could be a lot of money!

Thinking about it, I am also imagining our Christmas feast. There will be rice and peas, chocho, carrot, Irish potato, beetroot, calaloo; and, best of all, roast chicken. My stomach grumbles as I walk up to the library gate.

I slip inside the library. Miss Patterson is busy talking to Mr. Keene, the preacher. They're whispering about his Sunday sermon and a certain passage in the Bible.

I open up my book of national heroes, and right away, the page blurs and my mind wanders. For some reason, I cannot stop thinking of Brother John.

Last Sunday, he trimmed hair, as he always does. This is an afternoon ritual with him. The whole neighborhood gathers, one at a time, to get their hair cut by Brother John in Mama Poon's yard.

They sit under the big ackee tree, and he trims, his scissors singing all through the long golden afternoon.

At this time, I am the only one in our family who's allowed in Mama Poon's yard. If Johnny, Bup, Tonyskank, or the girls try to come inside the fence, Mama Poon will greet them with a hard green almond. And, let me tell you, she can throw like a pro.

The only exception to this rule about the yard is on Sunday when it's hair-trimming time. Then, after everyone else's hair is trimmed, she allows us to enter and have ours done too. Brother John has always trimmed hair in someone's yard.

When the afternoon shadows are long in the dark green Bermuda grass, we walk through Mama Poon's gate, single file. Brother John, who has been talkative and friendly all day, trims his own family in silence. Never a word, for any of us. And if you say something to him, he acts like he doesn't hear you. Except for the fact that his hands are gentle, you'd think he hated us.

On the porch, the whole time, Mama Poon eyes us. She never says anything either. But her eyes talk all the while. She sits in her straight-back chair, idly smoking Craven-A cigarettes, and staring coldly.

Brother John doesn't play tarantula with his hand this time. He's as sober as a post and serious as a john crow vulture.

Miss Patterson interrupts my thoughts. Mr. Keene goes out the door with a brisk nod. Miss Patterson sits down next to me with a little sigh, and opens the book she is holding very carefully.

The book is old, the pages smelling of sea salt, cedar wood, and mildewed years.

Miss Patterson's eyes are gleaming behind her eyeglasses.

"This book," she explains, "has much to say about Jonkonnu."

She glances at me, knowingly.

Her eyes seem to say: the whole town knows about *you*, and it is proud, the town is proud.

I smile back at her. Her face tightens.

"– is not just a dance," she informs. "Jonkonnu is a play. A passion play. A mummery, you know."

I don't know what any of these things are.

She turns some pages of the book, and the paper is like old silk, smooth and cool to the touch.

"Look here," she says.

The book is called *Sketches of Character in Illustration of the Habits, Occupations, and Costumes of the Negro Population in the Island of Jamaica, Drawn After Nature, and in Lithography.*

Miss Patterson speaks softly, silkily, her well manicured, nail-polished index finger sliding down the page.

"– is not just gourd rattle, fife, toot, triangle, and tambourine noise, Tall T. Jonkonnu is an old African thing. Read up on it, Little Brother John, so you can know why we're so proud to have a man like your father, and why we're so glad you are going to be with him at Jonkonnu."

Then she gets up, and, her dress whispering, goes back to her desk. Which leaves me wondering ... how could a whole town love Brother John so? I mean, he's a man, who, at the drop of a nut, quits his wife and children to go live in the house of an obeah woman.

How can they love such a man?

How can I?

Chapter 15

When I first showed up at the library, Miss Patterson told me, "Stop reading out loud!" However, as the weeks go by, I stop using my finger to mark my place. I learn to read with my mouth shut.

Then I really begin to enjoy reading silently, the words racing pell-mell through my mind, the images taking me spinning by surprise. I am really hooked. I even like the smell of books — each one is a little different. And if a book *smells* good, I am sure to like the words printed on the inside of it.

Take this Jonkonnu book, for instance. I thought I knew all there was to know about Jonkonnu. But that's what I'm saying about books. There's so much more to learn.... take the word *Jonkonnu*. It comes from the Ewe people of Eastern Ghana and Togo. *Dzon konnu*, the book says, means sorcerer. And it also says the dance is done to bring back the ancestor spirits.

I discover that Jonkonnu dancers used to carry a boat as they danced. Later on, in the New World, this boat, or ark, was the headgear of a single dancer.

Several feet high and made out of palm fronds, the headpiece sort of celebrated Noah's finding dry land.

Maybe so.

I ask Miss Patterson if this could really be true.

She raises her eyebrows.

"Belisario's a foremost scholar," she tells me.

"But the book was published in *eighteen thirty-seven*."

Miss Patterson taps the table with her pencil.

"What's *that* supposed to mean?"

"It not – *modern* – Miss Patterson."

"Neither," she says, "are *we*."

"It say here," I tell her, "that one time the colonial government shut down Jonkonnu."

Miss Patterson nods. "I remember reading that."

"Then whole of Kingston have a great big fight. They call it the John Canoe Riot."

Miss Patterson taps her pencil on her desk blotter. She smiles.

"After that," she says, "the government let the dance go on."

"And them never take it away again?"

She nods. Miss Patterson points her pencil at me. "You read that right, but you say it wrong. You must say *they* never take it away, not *them*."

I nod my head and say, "They."

"Yes," she adds. "The governor figured that the dance was out of hand, you know. The people had put all kinds of masquerade into it. They were making fun of the *bull buckra*, the big plantation owner. That's when the governor shut down the celebration. But the people wouldn't stand for it, and so they rebelled against it, and back came the Jonkonnu."

"Some of that funmaking is still in Jonkonnu."

Miss Patterson kisses her teeth, chuckles.

"Yes, mon. Of course, Jonkonnu lives on and on. Why do you think we like it so?"

"Because there's so much *history* in it."

"*Our* history."

"Maybe," I muse, "maybe, one day, I'll write a book about Jonkonnu."

Miss Patterson takes off her eyeglasses and laughs.

"They say, 'who feel it, know it,' and *you*, Likkle Brother John, *do* feel it."

I go out of the library into the bright white heat.

Can everyone see that, one day, I will write a book?

Chapter 16

Before Jonkonnu the men go to the top of Tank Lane and sit by the old water tank. In the pearl soft shadows, they wait for Brother John. As treasurer, I'm allowed to go to their rehearsals. No one else from the village is there, just me.

And the night magic.

I sit opposite Busha Green's Rum Shop, where the men buy dark Guinness and Dragon Stout. The little turn in the road, where the shop is and where the men practice, is called Canoe Pond Road. I take my place where I can see everything, sitting on a chunk of reef rock.

As I chew on a june plum, the men come out of the dusk, their musical instruments mute in their hands. They sit on the wire grass under the water tank, waiting for Brother John in the gloomy yard shadows.

Sticky, with his snare drum and his kindly, saintly face. I like him because he's friendly and fatherly, but also for his talent. His drum hangs on a strap that goes around his shoulder. When he walks the drum makes a little tattling noise as the tight head responds to his footsteps. *Tat-a-tat, tat-a-tat.* Back straight, Sticky sits beside Lucky Hill, the fifeman. Lucky lays down a flutey melody, which Sticky follows with his guava sticks. The two men are a matching set, now sitting, now strutting as if into some ancient, unknown battlefield.

Bosun, the comical, big-belly man. He's throwing his weight around and moving on small, pointy feet. Loud and swaggering, he's the front-line act, the man who makes comedy out of mime. He and Brother John are best friends, Bosun being a sort of a second lieutenant down at the docks.

On Jonkonnu day, Christmas morning, Bosun will be a star. But until then – and all the rest of the quiet work-a-day year – he is just Brother Hog. A man who eats too much, keeps to himself, and has small greedy eyes. It isn't until he dons his striped short-sleeve sailor's shirt and bosun's cap that he becomes our favorite clown. All the *pickneys* love him and they can't get enough of his fool-fool ways.

Now Bosun is darting about, piggily. Mimicking the neighborhood noises. A goat blats, he picks it up. A car horn honks, he imitates it, crudely, on purpose.

I have to laugh at Brother Hog; I can't help it.

Clappy's joining in too. With his washboard and thimble fingers, he's setting up a rhythm that links to Sticky's drum and Lucky Hill's flute. Clappy's a bag of bones next to Bosun; and to see the two of them together causes instant laughter.

Nonetheless, Clappy's a most important member of the group. His thimble fingers attack the corrugated grooves of his washboard – *sh-shup, shshup, sh-shup*, and *clackety, clack*. How perfectly he keeps time with that fife and drum.

Red, the Indian man, is a fellow I've always liked to look at. As the Crown, he struts about in an assortment of patched together, kingly, castaway clothes, covered with little round hanging mirrors. Unsmiling and poker-faced, Red hardly ever talks. It's his royal uniform that gets the kids going on Jonkonnu day. The tiny mirrors burning all over his wiggily, jiggly body. His frightful, foolish, strutful, shimmying dance is laughable, but there is something a little frightening about it too.

Plus, Red carries a small hatchet like a scepter. The children always sense danger when they see Red, and they run away. Afterward, when the dance is over, they beg to touch his mirrors and fringes. He lets them too, smiling warmly for the first time.

At the top of Tank Lane hill, by the old dripping water tank with the creeper vines hanging down, the rehearsal's begun. However, it won't officially start until Brother John gets there – and he *still* hasn't showed up.

The *peenies* are flashing through the veils of thickly forested hills. I see their glowing tails, trailing through the darkness. In my ears, the high clear piping song of the Chinee tree frogs. *Cheerio, cheerio*, they sing along with the musical instruments, as if they too were a part of it.

Then, Brother John appears.

He's so large, coming out of the pitchy patch night, monstrous. My heart shudders when I see him. Why am I so frightened of my own father? His great bare chest is shining in the half-light.

He is so dark, my father. Not in skin only. But it's like he's a part of the night, the Jonkonnu, and so many nameless things.

Then too Brother John doesn't really belong to me anymore — not the way he used to. He's a stranger whom we have known all of our lives. A stranger, who, despite our love for him, is now stranger to us than ever before.

Huge, strange, towering Brother John. Is this what gets my heart pounding? His hugeness, his strangeness? Or just that he is no longer mine?

Brother John sits upon a rock that is like his throne. Hands resting on knees. Shrouded in darkness, his eyes are open, unseeing.

When he speaks, his voice is so low he makes the other men sound, and seem, like choirboys.

"All right, Red," he says, for no reason.

Red stands taller when Brother John speaks to him. And straighter.

The round of greetings goes about in the little gathering. It doesn't include me because I am now off to one side, sitting on the reef rock with my back against the iron legs of the old water tank. I'm kind of hidden. I don't want Brother John to greet me just then, but at the same time I do.

"Bwai," he orders, "come outta de wet so me can see you!"

I step forward, my heart thundering in my chest.

The burning embers of cigarettes surround me. The air too is full of the men's smoke. The *peenies* dart through these bluish clouds.

Something hits me in the chest. Falls at my feet.

The lounging men laugh.

All but Sticky. He's close by, his guava drum sticks in his hands. I hear him say, "Good catch, Tall T."

I bend down and pick up whatever it is.

Then I know by the feel of it – it's the treasury bag. "If you catch dat bad, we gwan be poor," Brother John rumbles ominously.

Muffled laughter. Cigarette embers brightening, fading. Peenies soaring through the purple dark. My heart's jumping. The tree frogs are chiming.

Brother John looks at me; I feel his eyes burning like those cigarette ends. "Him catch good when him need to," Sticky offers.

Someone mumbles, "True, true."

Then, as if by some secret signal, the men are all alert and ready.

Brother John jumps up, stomping a hard beat. The rest of the men join in, clamorously.

The fife whistles.

The drum patters.

The grater rattles.

The men's voices are, all at once, singing.

The verses of their song are about the tower of flowers – the ark that was once worn on the head of an ancient Jonkonnu dancer. Once called Jock-O-Green, this dancer carried Noah's ark of flowers and ferns. The headdress went up, they say, to the moon. That is all gone now, but the men still sing of it, as if it happened yesterday.

"Starry, oh, starry, oh," the men sing in their lullaby voices, their arms swaying and swinging, arcing in the dark. They're moving rhythmically now, doing unseen footwork.

The village is listening; I can feel it.

I am so close to Brother John, and so far away.

Chapter 17

After the Jonkonnu rehearsal is over, I give the treasurer's bag to Brother John, but he won't take it. He brushes my hand aside, walks away from me. Then he disappears down the lane. Sticky walks home with me in silence, the tree frogs all around us, singing us home.

When we arrive at my house, Sticky pauses at the gate as I go in.

"Your time a-come, Tall T," he reminds me. He means of course that soon I will carry the purse and be a part of the pantomime myself. All eyes will be on me. My skin prickles when I think of it.

I wave to him and close the gate.

He rubs my head once, says, "All right, soon come."

The music of the Jonkonnu is in my head still, as I get ready for bed. Johnny is sound asleep, snoring. His arms and legs are everywhere. I don't know how I ever share that mattress with him, but I do.

On the other side of the room screen, the twins are sleeping. Even in sleep, they're orderly. Tonyskank and Bup are also asleep on their mattress.

I stuff the treasurer's bag under my pillow. Then I lie down, try to get comfortable. There is something troubling me up in the rafters.

It's a *rat bat*, the kind with the pushed-up face, that sleeps upside down. All the old people say that rat bats are a blasphemy to God because they offer Him their backside instead of their face. Anyway, we don't like rat bats, and it's my job and Johnny's – to chase them away.

I get up out of bed. Johnny blinks, yawns, sits up the moment he hears the thatch broom swishing over his head. He's taller, of course, and he knows there's only one way to scare a rat bat.

"Gimme that thing," he orders as he stands up in bed. I hand him the broom. He stretches up, and holding the end of the handle, Johnny whisks the broom this way and that. *Swisht.* The rat bat flutter-flaps down, and up, and to the side, zigging and zagging. Finally, it flies through the space between the rafters and the roof.

Johnny starts to laugh.

"Not so loud, Johnny."

"Did you see the way he tried to come back in, just before I smacked him?"

I chuckle, nodding.

"Hope he's over at Mama Poon's by now."

We both laugh at this, then settle down in bed.

In a few moments, Johnny is right off to sleep again. Leaving me in the darkness, wondering.

My mind is away and gone, up at the top of Tank Lane, jumping to the *grawk* of the grater and the *tack-tack* of the guava sticks.

Footsteps.

Iya comes to my bed. There's the faint smell of night jasmine outside the open window, and some little moonlight filtering in. Iya goes behind the twins' screen. I hear her tucking them in.

Then she returns to our part of the bedroom and looks at me. Iya whispers, it "Jonkonnu singing sweet tonight." She kneels down and sits on a corner of the mattress.

I reach under my pillow, pullout the treasurer's bag. She smiles.

"You see the bag?" I ask.

She doesn't respond. She keeps smiling in the moonlight. I know she's seen it though. I push the bag back under the pillow.

"Brother John," she whispers, him is a rough, rough man."

"I know that, Iya."

"And he has such rude ways."

"I know that too."

"But, Tall T, no matter what, you must remember this." She pauses, the moonlight silvering her high-cheekbone face.

I hear her breathing deeply in the stillness.

"He will always be your father. Remember that."
She looks at me directly. Her face is young, I think,
and pretty.

"You be proud of Brother John," she warns. "No
matter what he's done, or what he will do, or won't do,
in time to come. No matter what happen, you stand up
proud, and be a man."

I nod.

"Because," she continues in her gentle voice, "If it
not for Brother John, there be no Tall T."

After she leaves, I lie awake, thinking about this.

He is my father.

And I am his son.

But what is it that makes a man?

Is it the father before him?

The father before that?

Fathers all the way back to the Ark?

And before that?

Chapter 18

The sun comes up red as a poinsettia. I get dressed to the morning song of the birds in the yard. Singing in the wild cane and the custard apples, I hear baldpates, pea doves, blue quits, and banana katies. Our fruitful yard is full of their warbling and twittering, their feisty bickering.

I pull an my worn khaki pants, my old shortsleeve shirt. Outside in our tin-roof kitchen, breakfast is ready. Iya's made cornmeal porridge with sweet cream, topped with fresh-grated nutmeg. There's bag bread, guava jelly, and cheese; fry dumpling and plantain.

What a special breakfast!

And, because it's Jonkonnu day, Iya's made coffee-tea, fresh ground from the one coffee tree in the yard.

All in all, I feel I am ready.

The only thing that worries me is my trouser zipper – I have to remember to keep my shirttail in front of it.

Iya chuckles. "That *dibby-dibby* zipper's nothing but trouble. "Here," she offers, "this is a straight leather belt of Brother John's. He left it here, and I cut it down to size just for you, Tall T."

I slip it through the loops in my pants. It fits perfectly. The brass buckle in front sort of pins the zipper down.

"No one see the zipper now."

She grins and pats me on the shoulder.

"This is your day, Tall T."

After breakfast I begin to get nervous.

Johnny walks with me to the verandah. He stands there, stretching in the sunlight. Stretching and smiling.

A moment later Bup and Tonyskank join us.

Out in the street I see Auntie, waving at me.

And Mr. Nachasow, keeping his distance from her, but trying to see everything just the same.

I've got the treasurer's bag in my hand. Suddenly, it occurs to me that I shouldn't have it out in plain sight like this, so I tuck it into my heavy leather belt. The new belt feels important, strong and protective.

Now the Jonkonnu men are coming down Tank Lane. They aren't dancing or singing. They're stepping lively in the morning light, seeming like men from some ancient fable. In full costume, they come up to our gate.

Bosun walks mincingly with his funny striped sailor's shirt, which can't quite hide his bulging belly. He's wearing the cap with two little swallowtails hanging off the side. Already, he's burping and oinking, and making the neighbors call, *"Bo! Bo! Bo!"*

Lucky Hill's tootling away on his bamboo fife. He's wearing a brown suit and heavy leather shoes.

Sticky's got a full-sleeved shirt, a gold vest. His salt-and-pepper beard's finely trimmed. His snare drum hangs at his side on a leather strap, ready for action.

Clappy's fingers are agleam with silver thimbles, and though he looks just like a mosquito in his dark plain clothes, his fingers lend him a kind of magnificence.

Red's bronze hair is all matted on his head and flat like a helmet. He's got some outrageous fowl plumage sticking out of his capelike clothing. A string of feathers hangs down his back. He's fringed and fabulous, and ablaze with tiny round mirrors, winking in the sun.

I take my place at the rear of the troupe beside the one man who wasn't at rehearsal. His name's Bassy and he plays, naturally, the big bass drum, *ga-boom, ga-boom.*

I feel eyes of admiration on me and everyone in the group. I've never felt so important in my life.

Suddenly, there's a loud noise over at Mama Poon's, and Brother John bursts forth.

At first, the people pretend not to see him: it's bad luck to see the devil so early in the morning. But Brother John's not about to be missed. Mouths fall open as he swaggers out into the sunshine, swinging a goat's foot cane and wearing a shiny silk top hat. His feet are booted and cleated. His fine black suit, high-fashion coat and tails look waxed in the sun.

Underneath, though, he's got no shirt. And his big, hairless chest, dark black like his coat, ripples with muscle.

The high silk hat is cocked at an angle. Little goat's horns poke out the sides of his head. His gold-rimmed, black-lens sunglasses glitter. With them on he has no eyes and this makes his face all the more evil. Down Tank Lane he sings, "*Oh deah de dawn, oh, Martin, oh feah deah dawn, oh.*" This morning song's always sung when the Jonkonnu men start out. I've heard it many times, but I've never been a part of it as I am today. My lips mouth the words, though my voice is too shy to sing them.

As we go down the hills toward Oracabessa, I notice Jerks with his sly grin. He's looking at me, enviously. Belling too, wide-eyed wishing he were — shall I say it? — in my shoes.

Mr. Lenny is frowning and when he sees me, he breaks into a grin. Miss Patterson's looking fully at me, her shoulder bag bulging with books. She gives me the hardest stare of all, yet I know she's the proudest of all. Buddy Simms gives me a big hearty wave as we go on down the road.

We head toward Ocho Rios on the Queen's Highway. It's a few miles before the road levels out past the racecourse, and then another five before the bend of Walker's Wood and Fern Gully where we will go straight into town. The sun is hot on my shirt, the sweat wetting up my pants.

How can Brother John, in his heavy, dark clothes, move so swiftly through the heat? By the time we're out in the treeless country where there's nothing but rock, cow, and grass, he's moving along like a locomotive. The sun is hammering our heads. Brother John is steaming forward, his feet clicking musically on the glimmering road to Ocho Rios, city of eight rivers.

We pass a broken-down Great House – one of those two-storied, tin-roofed estate houses from slave times. In tough red dirt yards, little children squat under almond trees, pounding nuts with stone mashers. Old, white-bearded men glare at us from rusted wrought-iron gates. Behind them the Great House sags in the sun like a strange dream.

Soon the road comes to the Blowhole, where the sea spouts out of the rocks and roars whitely in the air. We pass it by without slowing our step, following the coast to White River, where bamboo shacks appear on the roadside, and the sellers of coconut water offer us greetings – but we never stop. Brother John's way out ahead of us still. My mouth is dry and I'd dearly love to tilt a water coconut; to spill the sweetness down my hot throat. But I know there'll be no refreshment until we're done for the day.

We come at last to White River Bay, Glitter Beach, Shaw Park Beach. At each of these places, people greet us with cries of joy. Everywhere, the Christmas crowds are gathering. Finally, Brother John stops. And, with a nod of his black top hat – and no hesitation – the dance begins.

Chapter 19

As the crowd gathers around I crouch under the shade of a flamboyant tree. The people are pressing closer to the Jonkonnu troupe. Men, women, and children are pouring out of the earth, until, wherever you look there are faces, faces, faces.

Now Sticky rattles his drum, Lucky Hill tootles his flute. But Red just stands there like a statue in the park. Then, all at once, he starts to shimmy and shake, and from beneath his fringed shirt, he pulls out his hatchet. The children run and hide then, peeking from behind the safety of their mothers' dresses. Red's terrified them with his whirling mirrors, his famous hatchet, his blank stare.

Clappy and Bosun dodge each other, jigging back and forth, weaving in and out of the crowd. The people don't know where they're coming from, or where they're going next. Clappy's grater goes *chrrrrr*. Bosun belches and bumbles. These two comedians make everybody laugh. But the wandering eye keeps coming back to the dead serious face of Red and his hatchet.

In the desperate excitement, no one sees that Brother John's disappeared. He's slipped away behind the trunk of a fig tree.

Now, when the troupe's worked everyone into a furor, out comes the devil himself. He jumps into the air, arms spread, tails flying, children scattering.

Women back up, fanning themselves with folded Gleaner papers. Men stare, motionless, trying to hide their feelings. No doubt, though, they like the spectacle as much as anyone does. Also, no doubt, all eyes are riveted on the devil.

It's his size, for one thing. You can't overlook a seven-foot devil in a swallowtail suit and top hat. Not to mention, he's flim flamming all around, leering, lunging, swiping the air with his goat's foot cane. Sometimes, he hops on one leg, then hops on the other, then ducks down, arms at his side, and dives for the children.

This rush is followed by a counterattack, Sticky drumming madly, Clappy going *cht-cht-cht-cht*, making a hurricane rain on his washboard. And, all the while, Red's twitching to the beat – eyes closed with hatchet in hand – and Bassy's walking in circles, *ga-boom, ga-boom*, with his enormous bass drum.

The crowd's pushing back now, thronging to get away from the dangerous antics of Brother John.

Any moment now, I feel, the whole thing's going to explode. And so it does. The Jonkonnu stops so abruptly, it's like a passing storm.

It fades before our eyes.

Then the people start flinging coins, as if the trees were raining money. I dive for each one, for if I don't get there quick enough, a beggar will beat me to it.

I move like a mongoose, snatching every last penny.

The Jonkonnu men are already on the move, going up the road. They leave me behind in the rain of coins. Two little boys are helping me.

A beggar comes out of nowhere, stabs at a silver coin – gets it. Cackling, he flashes a quarter in my face. His pink tongue wiggles like a worm in the dark cave of his mouth.

I pay him no mind. I have to hurry to catch up. The men are almost around the bend, out of sight.

Giving my helpers a nickel each, I pour a fistful of coins into the treasurer's bag. My hands tremble, I take a deep breath, try to steady myself. There's an uneasy feeling about carrying such a weight of money. But I loop the leather strings of the bag onto my belt, and run to catch up with the troupe.

For the rest of the day, we trudge from one part of Ocho Rios to the other. Everywhere we go, it's the same. The mystified faces, the screaming children – Brother John always making his jumpy entrance from behind a tree. Bosun, belly pushed out, burping his way around the crowd. Red, quivering like an almond leaf, hatchet gleaming. Clappy, grating and shaking. Sticky drumming, Bassy booming.

The day goes by, but no one notices, or seems to notice, the devil's treasurer. I'm kind of like a *money-duppy*, a ghost of the woods. I'm just there to do my thing and disappear.

At the end of the masquerade, I scurry to catch coins. And there's always a beggar, teaching me his trade, moving faster than I do. There's always a helper too, whom I reward with a nickel.

Then, my bag bruising my wrist, I run to catch up with the others.

The day drags on. I'm hungry. The sellers of roast chicken and breadfruit are always beckoning. The cooking smells are rich and flavorful, wafting in the air. The half barrels full of pimento coals are always smoking. The meat, dripping and sizzling.

However, I'm always hurrying to catch up to the Jonkonnu men, who never stop to eat. They just push on, working the market, the run-down, rickety alleyways where the money's thrown into the mud, and I've got to dig it out with my finger nails. Higglers hollering everywhere, the treasurer's bag growing fuller and fuller, heavier and heavier.

And all eyes upon it!

By day's end, I'm no longer invisible – I am, in fact, a point of interest! A boy with a bag of riches that any beggar would like to steal. My eye searches them out, however. Once, a boy, taller and stronger than I, dashes from behind a bamboo *tuckshop*, and tries to grab the bag. I see him making his move. Before he can strike the bag like a shark, I raise my fist and swing the heavy sack of coins against the side of his head. He goes down hard. By the time he gets up on his feet, ready to fight me, Sticky's there to help. "Mind yuhself, bwai, or yuh get puppa-lick." The boy doesn't wait around to see if Sticky'll do it. He runs off.

"You all right, Tall T?"

"Everything cool," I tell him.

"Easy."

Brother John says, "You almost get broke, bwai. Yuh no strong nuff fi carry dis bag?" It's no small thing to have the devil, in black tail and horn, eyeing you, cursing you. And when the devil's your own father, it's worst of all. However, he stalks off and that's all he says to me for the rest of the day.

We work until nightfall. Never resting, never eating. A couple times, we take a drink from a standing pipe. Once from the bamboo pipe outside of Ocho Rios by the Bauxite dock and another time in the cool ferns by Mammee Bay.

Back in Ocho Rios, people are filling their mouths with roast corn, meat patties, bammy, and golden fry fish. But we have none. My belly's making noises like Bosun's, but no one can hear it except me. Or so I think. Sticky asks, "Tall T you starve, mon?" He offers me a roti, a rolled-up piece of Indian flatbread that he has with him. I swallow it whole. He buys me a bottle drink too.

I feel Brother John's disapproval, but he doesn't say anything to us.

After it gets dark and there aren't any more crowds on the street, I figure we'll stop and finally eat something.

However, I'm wrong. Brother John takes off his top hat, wipes his forehead with a handkerchief. Then he shimmies out of his swallowtail coat. All he has on now are his suspenders, (what we call braces) pants, and boots.

We're standing in front of Fisherman's Bay. Back in the cool banana leaves, there's a little shop where a lady sells fish tea. You can smell the aroma from way up on the road. My belly grumbles again.

Brother John says, "Make we see the bag, now."

He says this, not to me, but to Bosun.

Chapter 20

"Oh, boy!" Bosun squeals when he sees how fat the treasurer's bag is. Sticky laughs, and then the rest of them, but Brother John stands with his arms folded. Shirtless, he glowers at me. Sticky lights a match and sets a dry banana leaf to flame.

Bosun kneels down, pours the money on to the hard-packed earth. Clappy goes away into the darkness, returning a moment later, with a kerosene bottle lamp he's borrowed from someone. The light casts away the shadows. Sticky stamps out the banana leaf. Brother John remains in the dark, watching over us. I'm too nervous to look at him. But I feel him like a cloud that covers the moon.

"Bosun, count the money, mon," Brother John rasps.

Bosun begins the tally. Coins line up in stacks. One after another.

I feel my sore wrist where the heavy bag has dragged all day long. It hurts, but no worse than my calves, my knees, my back. I want to sit down, but I'm afraid if do, I won't be able to get up again.

Now the coins, perfectly columned up in rows, are laid out for all to see. The kerosene bottle lamp flickers. The faces of the Jonkonnu men are washed in a golden glow.

I wonder what my wage will be – how much I've really earned.

And, when, when will I ever get something to eat?

Grunting, Bosun gets up. Pen in hand, he scribbles on a crumpled piece of brown bag paper.

Then he hands the total to Brother John, who steps into the swimming light. Brother John glances at the numbers, hands the paper back to Bosun.

My heart jumps in my chest. I can't read either of their faces. Is the money not enough? What's wrong?

My belly grumbles.

"Aw right." Brother John sighs hoarsely.

No one says anything.

Some of the men look away, eyes to the long ribbon of road, the road home.

What's going on? I can't figure it out. It seems like everybody wants to leave, and no one wants to get paid.

"Awright," Red echoes shiftily. His mirrors spark in the bottle lamplight. Then, mysteriously, he shrugs and just wanders off into the night.

Next, Lucky Hill walks out of the circle of light, dissolves away without a gesture.

Then, Clappy, Bassy. They each wander off, neither together, nor apart. Brother John looks down at me for the first time.

"Go home, bwai."

I don't know what to do. I look for Sticky, who's standing nearby. My heart's pounding.

Bosun's small piglike eyes are on me. He chuckles and grunts. Brother John steps over to Sticky and says something I can't quite hear. Whatever it is, Sticky sighs, and moves off toward the road. I see him under a long, slender, tall Panama palm tree. Looking at me. He nods his head, then he starts the long walk home. His drumsticks are in his back pocket. His drum vibrates with each step until he's out of earshot.

I can't believe he's going home without me. Brother John snaps, "Me say, go home. You hear?"

Slowly, I turn and walk away. He's going to call me back ... I can hear his outrageous laughter ... this is just a devil's joke ... he's going to call me back ... they're all coming back ... we're going to have a celebration ... a feast at Fisherman's Beach ... I can almost feel Brother John's arm around me ... I can almost hear him say that I did a good job ... I'm a good boy, who did a good job ... he's going to rub my head the way he used to ... he's going to, I know he is....

He does nothing.

When I reach the road, I look back, just once.

Brother John and Bosun are joined up, as always, and they're walking toward Fisherman's Beach. They're laughing and talking. Brother John's swinging the treasurer's bag. The last thing I hear is Bosun's grunt chuckle, Brother John's belly laugh.

I am out on the road, alone. In the dark.

I walk a ways, not believing what's happened.

On the other side of Ocho Rios by White River, I see a man sitting on a piece of logwood. "Yes, Tall T," comes the warm, familiar voice.

I step off the road and Sticky gets off the log to greet me.

He has a bag, which he gives to me right away.

I peer inside. Even in the dark, I can see he's picked up an orange, a ripe banana, and a large piece of *bulla bread*.

"Thanks, Sticky."

I fall into the food, eating hungrily as we walk.

When I've finished the last crumb of the dry, sweet bulla, Sticky suggests we stop at the bamboo pipe just up ahead.

I take a long, cool drink. It seems the bubbly water goes straight from my throat all the way down to my toes, refreshing my body and soul.

"That better?" Sticky asks, after drinking and wiping off his wet beard.

"I feel a little better ... a lot better."

"You have quite a day, Tall T."

We walk, thereafter, in silence, passing Banana Walk with the pewter-colored banana leaves, motionless in the thick moonlight. We pass Boscobel, Race Course, and then we are nearly home.

At Tank Lane, Sticky excuses himself, saying he has somewhere to go.

I ask, "Will we ever see any of our money?"

Laughing, he pats me on the back. "He paid us down at the beach, the way he always does. That's the deal, he and Bosun divide what they say is theirs, and afterward, he splits up the rest. Then, as you know, he goes to the bone dice."

"But what about my share?"

Sticky strokes his beard thoughtfully. "He didn't give you *nothing*?"

I shake my head.

"He *will*, Tall T."

I feel tears begin to well up in my eyes. Then Sticky reaches into his pocket and takes out a few dollars.

"Will this hold you over until Brother John comes home?"

I shake my head.

"Brother John doesn't come home anymore."

"Well, take the money, anyway."

There's no point in not taking it; after all, I did my job, didn't I?

As if reading my mind, he says to me, "You worked harder than anyone, Tall T. You can be proud of that."

He rubs my back with his warm, callused hand, and turns off toward the center of town.

It's late when I close the gate behind me. Mama Poon's lantern is still lit, but the other houses are dark. Iya meets me at the door.

I tell her I'm tired, but not hungry, which is the truth. For, somehow, I've lost my appetite.

Iya watches me take off my clothes.

I don't have to tell her; she knows.

But she asks, "Is that rough, rough man your father still?"

I want to answer her, but I don't know what to say. I want to tell her all the things that happened, but I have no words to explain. I want to tell her that Brother John is not just a devil in disguise, he's *really* the devil. But I'm too, too tired to talk.

I stretch out on the cool sheet. Johnny stirs, turns once. His feet, as usual, hang off the mattress.

Iya starts to leave the room.

"Brother John's me father still," I mumble, and fall to sleep.

Chapter 21

We don't see Brother John for several days. Then, when we do see him, it's as before, with Mama Poon standing on her porch, and Brother John dressing in the yard and running off to work.

As for the money, there is none. Not from him, anyway.

However, I get a big surprise Monday when a letter comes for Johnny and me. We eagerly open it and see that it's from our Canadian friend, Bernard.

Dear Johnny and Uton:

I am hoping that this finds you and your family well and happy from the holidays. It must be nice there at this time. Here, it is cold and snowy. I wish I were on the beach with you boys.

Do you remember the carvings you did for me while I stayed at Goldenhead Beach Hotel? Well, they are a great success! The hospital where I work has ordered an additional fifty coats of arms for Easter presents. I hope you can make them in time. I know it's a lot of work. Enclosed please find advance payment of $300. You can expect to see me at the hotel two weeks before Easter holiday.

Your friend, Bernard

Johnny and I are amazed and pleased at our great, good fortune. We read the letter over and over. Iya, when she sees it, says to me, "Surely, this is the money you were supposed to get from the Jonkonnu."

I ask what she means.

"Well, it says in the Bible what you sow is what you shall reap!"

"So, it doesn't matter where it comes from? I mean this man hardly knows us."

"But he understands us better than your own father."

I see the truth of that, though it is still a little hard to believe.

Johnny says, "The Father makes sure everyone got a father somewhere."

"– is true," Iya replies. "Now, you boys should be proud of what you have done. What other children could do so much, for so many, in so little time?"

"Iya," I tell her, "you told us that if one of us bring a mango into the house, we better cut it into six pieces. And that is just how we live, and how we did this."

"It was for you, Iya," Johnny adds. "To show you how much you mean to us."

Although her eyes are misty, she doesn't cry. No, she never cries unless one of us has cried first. She cries with us, sometimes, when the hurt is so bad we can't measure it. But she doesn't cry alone.

That afternoon I go to the library, as usual, and I take down the huge, leather-bound Bible with the stamped, gilt-lettered cover and the musty pages, and I read for the longest time, soaking in the words.

Miss Patterson asks, "You read about the man, Job?"

I nod.

"You read about the man, Jonah?"

I nod again.

Her eyes widen behind the frames of her eyeglasses.

"You read about Moses, Abraham, Daniel?"

"Uh-huh."

"So, what are you reading now?"

"I am reading about the Jacob Ladder."

Miss Patterson sighs, removes her glasses.

"That is the most beautiful story in the whole book."

And, then, she comes closer to me, touching the page I am on with her perfectly manicured nails. A sweet fragrance of Kananga water perfume follows her movements.

Softly, she reads aloud from Genesis 28: Verse 12.

> *And he dreamed, and behold a ladder set up on the earth, and the top of it reached to heaven: and behold the angels of God ascending and descending on it.*

"That is my favorite part too," I tell her.

"Why, Tall T?"

I think about that, then tell that it's because the same ladder is here, in Oracabessa, only there are not any angels on it, just men.

"Ah," she says knowingly. "But, Tall T, don't you know, the angels of God are often just men, just normal men. It's how the Father does His work. It says in another verse — *And Jacob awaked out of his sleep, and he said, Surely the Lord is in this place; and I knew it not.* "You understand? He knew it not."

"I think so."

Miss Patterson smiles, and her lovely hand settles like a butterfly on my left shoulder. Tall T, have you ever climbed the Jacob Ladder?"

I shake my head.

"Well, if you want to know what kind of men, or angels, live on this earth, then you must find out for yourself. You must climb the Ladder."

"Have you ever climbed it, Miss Patterson?"

She smiles faintly, touching her red lips with her index finger once; then she returns to her desk and busies herself with cataloging new books.

After a while, I excuse myself; I'm going to do something I've never done before. I'm going to climb the Jacob Ladder.

Chapter 22

I walk down the marl road past Mr. Hopson's Lunch Shop, past Mr. White's hardware, and Mr. Walsh's bakery, where the sweet, warm aroma of *totos* or rock buns is so strong it makes my belly growl.

How many times has Johnny run in there and swiped one of the coconut halves drying in the sun?

I chuckle, remembering the last time I saw Mr. Walsh chasing after Johnny, his arms white with flour, his face in a rage. And Johnny, long-legged and clumsy, fumbling up the hill in back of the bakery. Munching and running, and trying to keep from laughing.

At the bottom of the road, I look up at the green tangle of vines. The Jacob Ladder is cut into the center of the clay cliff.

The banana men are singing behind me. I turn around, momentarily, seeing if Brother John's there.

He's rowing a boat out to *The Producer*, the British freighter. Those long, long arms sure can row. No one can beat that man in a boat. No one can beat him anywhere else, except at bone dice or obeah. In spite of it all, I can't help but feel some kind of pride whenever

I hear people speak admiringly of Brother John. It's just that, as a father, he's not ours, anymore.

Or is he?

I just don't know.

The Jacob Ladder awaits. I step into the fig gloom of overhanging leaves. Looking up, I see the clean stairs, chopped by machete into the cliff side. All the way from top to bottom the cable-like vines hang.

I grip one in my hand. It's smooth from use, polished like green ebony.

One pull. Then another.

Without my looking, my feet find the stairs.

And slowly, I dreamily hoist myself up. Ten ... twenty ... thirty feet and up, up into the jungle air. The docks fall far away behind me, the calls of the banana men waver and fade. It seems I am higher than I really want to be. I am ascending up to heaven. I can't see the sky. Everything is drowned in fig leaves.

I stop for a moment and catch my breath.

Suddenly, I slip and almost fall.

I grab a strong vine and cling hard. My cheek touches the cold clay. My eyes are shut.

The mourning doves in the trees above are cooing softly. I imagine they are angels, singing. Their wings brush the top of my head, the angels stirring as they ascend the Ladder, and descend, rising and falling without alarm, without so much as a sound except for the sweet cooing of their voices, giving me the faith of Jacob's birthright – that the earth, the very earth I cling to, is mine, is ours. No one can take that away from us, for God gave it to us, and it is ours.

I twist my head and open my eyes.

Behind me, the blue sea.

Above me, finally, the blue sky.

And, where the Ladder ends, the road begins, winding all the way up to Tank Lane.

I can hear the splintered cries of the little children in the school yard. Soon, I imagine, Belling will draw the bell rope for the end of recess.

I hear again Miss Patterson's calm voice, saying, almost singing, *"Surely the Lord is in this place; and I knew it not."*

A banana katy titters over my head.

Confidently, I pull myself up the last few steps, sixty feet above the beach.

I have climbed the Jacob Ladder.

Chapter 23

In the evening Sticky shows up at our door. He takes me to the river in back of our house.

Together, we hunt for crabs, crayfish, or river shrimp. Sticky shows me how to make a spear from the *bones* of an old umbrella. Sharpening the point on a rock, he readies himself for a dive, while I hold his bottle lamp over the black, cold, burny water.

Each time he surfaces, beard bright and wet, I take a fish off the point of that spear. He gets mullet and mudfish, mostly. But a few times, he appears with snook, all silver-sided in the lamp's glare.

Afterward, we have a feast together. He makes a wonderful fish tea with cornmeal dumplings, boil-banana, fish, and, for extra flavor, Sticky throws in a store-bought package of chicken soup.

As I am eating, I imagine that this is the very feast I'd hoped for when we were in Ocho Rios after the long day of Jonkonnu.

I look at Sticky. He is not my father. But he loves me just like a father, and I can feel his love deeply. Once again, I see myself climbing the Jacob Ladder.

The feeling that everything is going to be all right fills me from the tip of my toes to the top of my head, and I hear the soft twittering of the doves, and I know they are God's angels and that I too am an owner of the earth. Like Jacob.

As for Brother John, I cannot choose to do anything but love him. For, after all, he put me here. He gave me my place on earth. It is up to me now to do something about it.

And I shall, I shall.

Afterword

There is no end to my story. Like anyone's, it goes along with plenty of ziggy-ziggy twists and turns. However, you must know that as the years have passed, things have changed for me, mostly for the better.

Brother John moved away from Mama Poon the day that I climbed the Jacob Ladder. He went away from Oracabessa and all that he knew there. It may seem hard to believe, but I missed him all the time. What he failed to do as a father, we forgave him – after which we just loved him for what he was and for what we remembered before he moved next door. Well, he eventually settled in Kingston, where he met up with another woman. Sometime after this, he died. We were with him – all of the children – at the end.

We told Brother John that we loved him for being our father. He told us how much he loved us and how sorry he was for the trouble he had caused us when we were youngsters. He died peacefully.

Johnny never went back to school. Today he has a family, and he owns his own cab. I see him regularly, and we are best friends. Bup has a family too, and he runs his own shop on Tank Lane. He sells sodas and little things people need every day. Tonyskank lives in New York City; he is a musician and a carpenter. Merline and Maxine both have families. Merline lives in Oracabessa and Maxine lives in Kingston. Like Johnny,

I never went back to school, but I also never stopped reading. I live in Ocho Rios, Jamaica, and I drive my own cab just like Johnny does. Some people still call me Library Boy because of the way I used to read for days on end.

Life teaches lessons the hard way. Reading about life teaches those same lessons the easy way, so I will always be grateful to Miss Patterson for putting me on that righteous path, and I hope she reads this book too, for she is such a big part of it.

Iya used to say, "Never give up. You must always believe that there is a way out, a way up, a way to be whatever you need to be. With a little effort you can get there. But when you arrive, remember who got you there. It wasn't you alone. Be thankful for what the Father gives."

Everything Iya taught, I remember very well. Iya is in all that I do and all that I say, each and every day. And even though she passed some years ago, I know that she is proud of me for telling my story with Gerry's help because she helped us to write this book while she was alive.

Love your family, whoever they might be.

Uton Hinds
Oracabessa, Jamaica

Note

Obeah, West African sorcery, is still used in the Caribbean. It was once a way of protecting a village in time of war, but its use today is for personal as well as social purposes. A man, for instance, may employ an obeah man or woman to help him obtain a visa to travel abroad. Obeah might also be used to make someone fall in love or put a person under a spell. The negative force of obeah, so painfully felt by the Hinds family in this novel, took place in the 1960s. But it is not our wish to have readers think that the family's ordeal is uncommon or imaginary. The events described in this book did indeed happen and are still happening in parts of the Caribbean today.

Gerald Hausman
Bokeelia, Florida

Glossary

bag bread – bread in a plastic bag

bammy – a round, flat, fried cake made from cassava flour

buckra – boss, generally white

bulla bread – a thick molasses cake pressed down to cookie size and eaten as a snack

bumba – bottom, backside

bwai – boy

calaloo – West Indian variety of leafy vegetable similar to spinach

chocho – pale green vegetable in the squash family; *choyote* in Spanish

dibby-dibby – troublesome or chatty

duppy – ghost or spirit

fi – preposition meaning to or for

gwan – go on

likkle – little

mumma-lick – momma spank or smack given to a misbehaving child

obeah – West Indian witchcraft derived from Africa; please see authors' note.

patoo – owl

peenies – fireflies (also: peeny wally)

pickneys – children

puppa-lick – papa spank or smack given to a misbehaving child

rat bat – fruit bat common to Jamaica

tuckshop – tiny shacklike, roadside store, often tucked up into a hill

Related titles by Gerald Hausman

Doctor Bird
Duppy Talk: West Indian Tales of
Mystery and Magic
The Kebra Nagast (Introduction by
Ziggy Marley)
Time Swimmer

Books with Cedella Marley

56 Thoughts from 56 Hope Road
60 Visions
The Boy From Nine Miles
Three Little Birds
Plain and Simple Wisdom From 56
Hope Road

Gerald Hausman is the recipient of many honors and awards for his more than 70 books about folklore and other cultures. He has co-authored a dozen books about animals and animal mythology with his wife Loretta.

Uton Hinds whose nickname in Jamaica was Tall T is a man of many talents – cab driver, carpenter, cook and visual artist. He supplied the true story for *The Jacob Ladder* and the oil painting for the cover.

CPSIA information can be obtained at www.ICGtesting.com
Printed in the USA
LVOW060629110413

328210LV00001B/9/P